Super Fun Facts for Amazing Kids

1500+ Fascinating and Interesting Facts Book for Smart & Curious Kids about Awesome Science, Animals, History, Space, World and Everything

PUBLISHED BY
Theo Reese

Introduction

Facts are the air of scientists. Without them, you can never fly. –Linus Pauling

I have always had a curious mind and loved passing on random facts to everyone around me. I made a lot of friends this way, but the greatest joy has been sharing them with my kids and watching them pass them on to others. Their friends are always asking them random stuff and if they don't know the answer, they promise to get it for them. That's the thing about facts—if you know a few of them, it often makes you want to know more. It fuels your curiosity and builds intelligence, and it's a whole lot of fun!

Facts have opened doors for me, allowed me to meet new people, and learn much more than I could have ever imagined. In my opinion, allowing kids to explore and learn through fun facts ignites passions and lets them discover whole new worlds. They can't wait to share what they've learned with their friends and it often makes them some of the smartest kids around!

So, are you ready to become the smartest kid in your class? The one who has all the fun facts about anything and everything? What about you, parents? Are you ready to learn alongside your kids and astound everyone with your knowledge? Well then, let's get started on a journey of curiosity, laughter, and astonishing information that will make you the champion of fun facts among your family and friends!

For Parents

You may have purchased this book as a gift for your curious kid or as a way to pass long hours on a road trip. Whatever the case, you're helping your child engage more with the world around them.

Most kids spend their time on phones or other electronics, so encouraging them to engage with topics of science or history will help them later in life. Maybe try telling them a fact a day, or read this book together before bed. Together, you and your child can become experts on over fifty topics.

Positive reviews from wonderful customers like you help others feel confident about choosing this book. Sharing your happy experience will be greatly appreciated! I hope you enjoy the Super Fun Facts For Amazing Kids!

Happy Learning!

Table of Contents

Chapter1: Fantastic Food Facts

1.Did you know that potatoes and tomatoes are related? They both come from the Nightshade family and have 92% similar DNA, meaning they share a common ancestor (Sharma, 2012).

2.Raspberries and roses are cousins (Iseli, 2022). No wonder they both have thorns!

3.Pistachios, almonds, and pecans are not nuts but seeds of fleshy fruits called drupes (Mandl, 2020).

4.Honey never goes bad! Archeologists found 3,000-year-old honey in King Tut's tomb that was still edible (Geiling, 2013).

5.Globally, humans consume 11 billion pounds (5 billion kilograms) of food every minute of every day (Thomson, 2014).

6.The original version of ketchup did not have any tomatoes in it (Bentley, 2014)!7.Insects contain between 9.96 g and 35.2 g of protein per 100 g which is comparable to meat (Payne et al., 2015).

8.Bananas are the most consumed fruit around the world (Savchenko, 2020).

9.Brussels sprouts taste different now than they did 20 years ago! Scientists identified what made them bitter and breeders were able to remove it (Morris, 2023).

10.The country that consumes the most fast food in the world is the United States of America. Every American spends about $160 million per year on fast food (Ireland, 2022).

11.The potato chip was first made by George Speck in Saratoga, New York after his customer complained that his French-fried potatoes were too thick and soft (Belman, 2014).

12.Popcorn, one of the world's oldest snacks, was found in a 1,000-year-old Peruvian tomb (Butler, 2018).

13.Centuries before the chocolate bar was even invented, Europeans discovered the Mayans consumed savory hot chocolate in the early 15th century (Bilton, n.d.).

14.Each Oreo cookie has 90 ridges around the edge, 12 flowers, 12 dots, and 12 dashes (Mordoh, 2016).

15.The chocolate chip cookie was created by accident in the 1930s when Ruth Wakefield ran out of cocoa while baking cookies (Michaud, 2013).

16.The oldest burger franchise is White Castle which opened its first store in 1921 (Sulem, 2023).

17.The first "drive-thru" was opened at Red's Giant Hamburg in Springfield, Missouri in 1947 (Anaya, 2022).

18.There are 38 million possible combinations to be made at Subway (Cameron, 2018).

19.Chicken nuggets were invented in a laboratory at Cornell University in 1963 by Robert

C. Baker (Rotondi, 2021).

20. Speaking of chicken nuggets, the largest chicken nugget ever made weighed in at 20.96 kg (46 lb 3.34 oz). That's approximately 115 times larger than your average chicken nugget (Suggitt, 2022).

21. The beginnings of ice cream came from ancient China, where a mixture of rice and milk was packed in snow to create an early form of ice cream in 200 CE (Leakey, 2022).

22. Before ice cream cones, you could buy "penny-licks" which were small glass containers filled with ice cream (Moss, 2019).

23. Speaking of licks, it takes approximately 50 licks to finish one scoop of ice cream (Williams, 2022).

24. The first cafe in Paris, called Café Procope, introduced ice cream made from cream, eggs, milk, and butter to the public in 1660 (*The history of ice cream*, 2021).

25. The world's largest ice cream cone was just over 10 ft (3 m) high (Williams, 2022).

26. Carrots were originally purple and yellow (Parker, n.d.)!

27. Carotenemia is a condition caused by eating too many (orange) carrots, making your skin yellow (Campbell, 2010).

28. The vegetable with the highest water content is the cucumber which has a water content of 96% (Jaarsma, 2021).

29. Broccoli is technically a bunch of flower buds! That's why they call them florets (Burke, 2023).

30. Sweet potatoes are not a type of potato. They're not even related to potatoes (Labyak, 2018)!

31. There can be up to 30 insect fragments in 100 g of peanut butter (LaMotte, 2019).

Chapter2: Spectacular Space

32. Most people think space is silent but waves caused by magnetic and electric fields can be heard with the right equipment (Hatfield, 2018).

33. The observable universe is vast, spanning about 93 billion light-years in diameter (Tillman & Gordon, 2017).

34. According to astronomers, the universe is approximately 13.7 billion years old (Weintraub, 2012).

35. The largest known structure in the universe is the Hercules-Corona Borealis Great Wall, a vast cosmic structure stretching over 10 billion light-years (Gunn, 2020).

36. A light-year is the distance light travels in 1 year, approximately 5.88 trillion miles (9.46 trillion kilometers) (National Aeronautics and Space Administration, n.d.).

37. It's impossible to count all the galaxies in the universe but astronomers estimate anywhere between 100 and 200 billion galaxies from recent data (Gunn, 2023).

38. The Andromeda Galaxy is on a collision course with the Milky Way and is expected to merge with it in about 4 billion years (McClure, 2019).

39. Stars are made up of 75% hydrogen and 25% helium. This includes the Sun (Cain, 2017).

40. Every billion years, the sun becomes 10% more luminous. This means that it's getting hotter over time (Cain, 2016).

41. The planet Uranus is the only planet to spin on its side

(Stein & Howell, 2017).

42. Mercury is the planet with the longest day. One day in Mercury is equivalent to 1,408 hours (Erickson, 2017).

43. Venus and Mercury do not have moons (Howell, 2015).

44. An earthquake on Mars is called a marsquake (Choi, 2019).

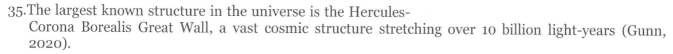

45. Jupiter emits more energy than it receives from the Sun (Owen, 2019).

46. The gravitational pull of a black hole is so strong, that not even light can escape from it (Kersting & Ruggiero, 2022).

47. In 2019 astronomers were able to take a photograph of a black hole thanks to the glowing gas left behind by matter the black hole consumed (Daniel Clery, 2019).

48. Once something gets sucked into a black hole, no one knows what happens to it (Kersting & Ruggiero,

2022)!

49. John Glenn was the first American to orbit Earth in 1962 and even managed to venture into space again in 1998 at the age of 77 (Lea, 2015).

50. Russian astronaut Valeri Polyakov holds the record for the longest time in space. He spent 437 days and orbited the Earth 7,000 times (Kekatos, 2023)!

51. If you are traveling to the Moon, it takes approximately 3 days to get there (Dobrijevic, 2023).

52. The fastest time to pass the Moon was achieved by the New Horizons probe on the way to Pluto. It passed the Moon in just 8 hours and 35 minutes (Dobrijevic, 2023).

53. There's junk in space! Due to space exploration, there are approximately 15,000 pieces of space debris larger than 4 inches (10 cm) in diameter (Gregersen, 2019).

55. It takes a minimum of 6 years to build a spacecraft (Newton, 2017).

56. The largest asteroid in space, Ceres, is also known as a dwarf planet and is approximately 27% the size of Earth's moon (Tedesco, 2019).

57. There are currently more than 1.1 million asteroids in the asteroid belt between Jupiter and Mars (Futterman, 2022).

58. Most asteroids are made up of rocks and rubble that have been around since the beginning of the solar system (Sausaiila, 2021).

59. Some asteroids in space have their own moons (Futterman, 2022).

60. Scientists sometimes call comets "dirty snowballs" because they're made up of ice, pieces of rock, and dust (Choi & Dobrijevic, 2021).

61. The largest crater on Earth is called the Vredefort crater and measures about 99 miles (159 km) in diameter (Baker, 2022).

62. The Sun is 400 times the size of the Moon! However, because It's 400 times farther away than the Moon, they appear as the same size (Cain, 2008b).

63. After you die, you can arrange to send your ashes into outer space (Letzter, 2016).

Chapter3: Astounding Animal Facts

Mammals

64. The smallest mammal is the bumblebee bat weighing just 0.004 lbs (2 g) and measuring a maximum of 1.3 in (3.3 cm) in length (Melina, 2016).

65. Hippos make their own sunscreen! They secrete a substance in their sweat that protects them from getting burnt in the sun (Vieagas, 2009).

66. Pangolins are the only mammals covered in scales (Dallas, 2020).

67. Humans and giraffes have the same number of bones in their necks (Sparks, 2020).

68. There are white bears in Canada! Known as the "spirit" or "ghost" bear, they belong to a subspecies of bears called Kermode bears (Shoumatoff, 2015).

69. There are approximately three sheep for every person in Australia! That's a whopping 67 million sheep (Ramel, 2019).

70. The patterns on a giraffe not only help with camouflage but also help to regulate the animal's body temperature (Leman, 2018).

71. An elephant's pregnancy lasts 22 months! That's almost 2 years (Montague, 2021).

72. Just as humans can be left or right-handed, elephants can be left or right-trunked (Dingfelder, 2023).

73. A gorilla's nose print is just as unique as a human's fingerprint (Sparks, 2020).

Predators

74. Orca or killer whale pods have different dialects, meaning that killer whales from one group may not fully understand another (Dayton, 1990).

75. A lion can stay without water for 4 days if need be (Johnson-Dollie, 2021).

76. African wild dogs have a kill rate of 85%, while lions have a kill rate of just 25% (Fair, 2021).

77. Don't think you're safe from a wolf in water! A wolf can swim up to 8 miles (13 kilometers) (Burns, 2019).

78. The predator with the largest bite force is the Nile crocodile. It has a bite force of 5,000 psi (Spanner, 2023). That is roughly over 20 times an average human's bite force.

79. Cheetahs were tamed and kept as pets and hunting companions by the ancient Egyptians (Harvey, 2018).

80. The largest animal on record that was eaten by an African rock python was a 150 lb (68 kg) hyena (Maxwell, 2023).

81. Grizzly bears are sometimes cannibals (Statt, 2023).

82. A bald eagle's grip is ten times stronger than ours, making it much easier for it to hold on to its prey in the air (Krug, 2023).

Birds

83. Hummingbirds have extremely fast heartbeats, ranging from 500 to 1200 beats per minute (Hannemann, 2022).

84. A bird's eye is often larger and heavier than its brain (Todoroff, 2015).

85. All birds can walk on land, but penguins are the only birds that walk upright (Hornsby, 2020).

86. There are poisonous birds found in Papua New Guinea called Pitohui that have poison on their feathers (Ligabue-Braun & Carlini, 2015).

87. Crows, and other members of the Corvid family, hold funerals for their dead (McMahon, 2022).

88. The cassowary is rated as the most dangerous bird in the world. It's able to kill humans with slashing blows of its feet (Elbein, 2021).

89. Birds can sleep while flying (Rattenborg et al., 2016)!

90. Flamingoes feed with their heads upside down so that they can filter their food (Ehrlich et al., 1988).

91. The Stresemann's Bristlefront of Brazil could be the world's rarest bird as only one has been seen in the wild since 2018 (Lisbon, 2021).

92. The white bellbird is the loudest bird on Earth! Its call reaches 125 decibels which is as loud as your typical rock concert (Frederick, 2019).

93. Recently, the record for the longest non-stop flight for a bird was set by a bar-tailed godwit that flew from Alaska to Tasmania—that's 8,425 miles (13,560 km) (Whitt, 2022).

Amphibians

94. The world's smallest frog is called the *Paedophryne amauensis* frog and is smaller than a dime (Newton, 2014).

95. The Mexican burrowing toad lives underground and only comes out when it rains or when it needs to breed (Beaudry, n.d.).

96. Contrary to popular belief, glass frogs are not see-through—only their underbellies are transparent (Gallagher, 2022).

97. Wood frogs freeze every winter and can stay frozen for 7 months, before thawing out in Spring (Netburn, 2014).

Reptiles

98. The leatherback sea turtle is the largest turtle in the world and the only one that does not have a hard shell (*Leatherback turtle | NOAA Fisheries*, 2019).

99. Crocodiles are found on every continent except Antarctica and Europe (Wingert, 2022).

100. The tuatara, native to New Zealand, has a "third eye" on the top of its head, which is not a true eye but can detect light and dark (Fritts, 2016).

101. Most geckos don't have eyelids. This is why they use their tongues to clean their eyes (Garcia, 2023).

102. Reptiles don't have sweat glands (Cornett, 2017).

103. Mexican beaded lizards and their cousin, the Gila monster are venomous lizards (Vallie, 2022b).

104. Garter snakes are not venomous. However, if you had to eat them, they would be poisonous since they store the toxins of their prey (Rafferty, 2019b).

105. There are 3,000 snake species in the world and only 15% of them are venomous (Meyers & Tadi, 2022).

106. There are more venomous snakes in Australia than non-venomous snakes (Cornett, 2017).

107. The Barbados thread snake is the smallest documented snake reaching a maximum length of just 4.1 in (10.3 cm) (Rafferty, 2012).

108. The gender of some turtles is determined by environmental conditions. Eggs exposed to low temperatures produce males and higher temperatures produce females (Gilbert, 2015).

Insects

109. The deadliest animal on Earth is the mosquito because of the diseases it transmits. Mosquitoes are responsible for a million deaths per year (Ross, 2021).

110. Butterflies taste with their feet (Fessenden & Krueger, 2020).

111. The giant Amazonian ant is the largest ant in the world and can reach 1.6 inches in length (Ward, 2021).

112. The water scorpion is not really a scorpion, it has a siphon that resembles a stinger. It uses this siphon as a snorkel to swim (Griffith & Gillett-Kaufman, 2021).

113. Dung beetles navigate via the Milky Way, using the pattern of light to roll their dung balls in a straight line (Dell'Amore, 2013).

114. Scientists have found that cockroach brains can be used to effectively treat bacterial infections. So, we might have cockroach brains in our meds soon (Ornes, 2010).

115. Honeybees have two stomachs. One is for eating and the other is for storing the water and nectar necessary to make honey (Keatley Garvey, 2018).

116. Termites like rock music! Since they use vibrations to determine the wood around them, rock music makes them eat wood faster (Hyde, 2020).

117. There are ants that can explode! They sacrifice themselves to distract an enemy so the rest of the colony can save themselves (Greenwood, 2018).

118. Caterpillars have 4,000 muscles. To give you some perspective, humans have 650 muscles (Hadley, 2019).

Marine Life

119. Did you know that coral can be used as bone graft material in humans? They have a similar composition to human bones (Demers et al., 2002).

120. Harlequin shrimp are sneaky hunters. These small shrimp flip starfish on their backs so they can't escape and then feed on them (Baker, 2020).

Dolphins

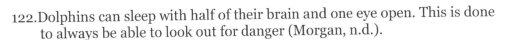

121. So far there are 40 dolphin species found in the world's oceans and rivers. An average dolphin's lifespan is around 50 years, and they can hold breath for 15 minutes.

122. Dolphins can sleep with half of their brain and one eye open. This is done to always be able to look out for danger (Morgan, n.d.).

123. Have you ever wondered why a dolphin's tail moves up and down and not side to side like most fish? It's because they evolved from land mammals whose legs were beneath their bodies (Klappenbach, 2019).

124. Dolphins are fast swimmers and can reach speeds of up to 20 mph (32 kph).

125. Orcas or "killer whales" are actually dolphins (*Orcas: Killer whales are the larges dolphin species*, 2010).

126. A bottlenose dolphin's brain weighs 3.5 lbs (1.6kg). That's approximately 0.7 lbs (0.3 kg) more than a human's (Grimm & Miller, 2012).

Sharks

127. Some sharks lay eggs! They're not typical eggs and have unique shapes. For example, Bullhead sharks produce spiral or corkscrew-shaped eggs (Osterloff, 2019).

128. Greenland sharks can live for over 400 years (Baker, 2020).

129. A shark's skin inhibits the growth of microbes that would make a shark sick. It's so effective that researchers are trying to apply it to hospital bandages (Heimbuch, 2012).

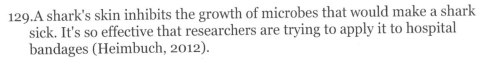

130. Dwarf lantern sharks are the smallest sharks in the world. They're rarely bigger than the palm of your hand (Diegor, 2022).

131. The fastest shark is the short-fin mako shark. It can reach speeds of 43 mph (70 kph) (BBC Wildlife Magazine, 2023).

132. Galeophobia is the overwhelming fear of sharks (Murphy, 2023).

133. The chance of you being attacked by a shark while at the beach is 1 in 3.75 million (McLaughlin, 2023).

134. Sharks also get cancer (Main, 2013).

135. Bull sharks are capable of living in saltwater and freshwater (Márquez,

2023a).

136. Sharks have been around for approximately 420 million years, making them older than Mount Everest (Joel, 2016).

Whales

137. A humpback whale's tail is just as unique as a human's fingerprint (Mackenzie, 2023).

138. A Narwhal is known as the "unicorn of the sea" because of its tusk, which is actually a tooth (Hall, 2017)!

139. Baleen whales, like the humpback and gray whale, have baleen plates instead of teeth. These plates are used to filter small organisms from the water (Kuhns, 2023).

140. Sperm whales have the largest brains out of all animals. Their brains are approximately five times the size of a human's (Mackenzie, 2023).

141. Humpback whales don't eat for 5–7 months out of the year (Koch-Schick, 2022).

142. Sperm whales sleep vertically underwater (Sullivan, 2023).

143. Many whale species undertake long-distance migrations between feeding and breeding grounds. The gray whale, for example, migrates over 10,000 mi (16,000 km) annually (*Gray whale,* 2019).

Fish

144. The ghost fish is currently the only fish seen at a depth of almost 27,000 ft (8,135m) in the Mariana Trench (Baker, 2020).

145. The biggest fish in the ocean is actually a whale shark. They can grow to 40 ft (12.2 m) (NOAA Fisheries, 2018).

146. Catfish in Albi, France have evolved to hunt pigeons. They're not alone either; tigerfish in Schroda Dam, South Africa jump out of the water to snatch swallows mid-flight (Spindler, 2022).

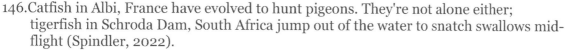

147. Fish have tastebuds both inside and outside their bodies (Lehnardt, 2016).

148. The electric eel is capable of producing electrical discharges of up to 600 volts. It uses this ability for navigation and to stun prey (Matthews, 2009).

149. The stone fish is the most venomous fish in the world. They are covered in spines that contain a toxin (Sackett, 2013).

150. The anableps, or four-eyed fish, is able to see above and below water at the same time (Avery & Bowmaker, 1982).

151. Some species of parrotfish produce a mucous cocoon around themselves at night. This bubble helps mask their scent, protecting them from predators while they sleep (BBC Wildlife Magazine, 2022).

Farm Animals

152. Horses can't vomit! They have a one-way digestive system that prevents food from being regurgitated (Funnel, 2022).

153. A dairy cow can produce 2,500 gallons (9,464 liters) of milk a year and 10–25 gallons (38–95 liters) of saliva a day (Giffen, 2021).

154. The tallest cow that ever lived was an incredible 6 ft 2 in (1.9 m) tall (Newman, 2023).

155. Sheep and goats only have teeth on their lower jaws. They grind their food with their hard palates (Giffen, 2021).

156. Think you sweat like a pig? Probably not, since pigs don't actually sweat at all (Ingram, 1965).

157. To produce a dozen eggs, a hen has to eat approximately 4 pounds of feed (Gabriel, 2017).

158. Miniature donkeys only grow to 36 in (92 cm) from hoof to shoulder and weigh less than 400 lbs (180 kg) (Bradford, 2016).

159. All ducks have waterproof feathers (Gaeng, 2022a).

160. Goats have rectangular pupils, providing them with a wide field of vision to detect predators (Bradford, 2015).

161. Counting sheep does not actually help you sleep! The saying may come from the fact that sheep herders could not sleep until they counted all their sheep to ensure that none were missing (Gibson, 2017).

Pets

162. Dogs have three eyelids (Marmurek, 2022).

163. Cats spend 30% of their time awake grooming themselves (Noble, 2023).

164. It's possible to keep a skunk as a pet! They are incredibly friendly creatures when raised from a baby but most people have their scent glands removed (McLeod, 2003).

165. Dogs have 100–300 million scent receptors, compared to a human's 5–6 million (Kelley, 2022).

166. Creme Puff, a cat from Texas, was the oldest cat who ever lived. The cat lived for 38 years and 3 days (Shah, 2023).

167. It's illegal to own a pet hamster in Hawaii (Gerkensmeyer, 2022).

168. Teacup pigs do not exist. They are regular potbellied pigs that are smaller than standard farm pigs, growing up to 200 lbs (91 kg) instead of 1,000 lbs (454 kg) (Donnelly, 2019).

169. If you get a hedgehog as a pet, keep in mind that they are nocturnal! They'll be up all night while you sleep (McKinnon, 2018).

170. A student in Mexico breeds Flemish Giants which are the largest rabbit breed in the world. His current bunnies weigh around 20–23 lbs (9–10 kg) and are similar in size to small dogs (Milan, 2023).

171. If you keep goldfish in the dark for a prolonged period, it will turn white (Stanton, 2015).

New Species

172. Approximately 18,000 new species are discovered every year! Considering there are many places in the world left to be explored, this number won't be decreasing anytime soon (Peters, 2023).

173. There have been 5,000 new species identified around an untouched area of the Pacific Ocean! Most of the new species are unique to the area and are not found anywhere (McVeigh, 2023).

174. There has been a new anemone found off the coast of Japan that only lives on the shells of hermit crabs, Called *Stylobates calcifer*. This anemone makes the crab look as if It's decorated with flowers (Greenwell, 2023).

175. A new snake species was named by the actor Leonardo DiCaprio this year. The DiCaprio snail-eating snake is found exclusively in the jungles of Central and South America (Shersby, 2023).

176. A dried specimen of the waterlily was in Kew's herbarium for more than 170 years before being identified as a new species in 2022 (Greenwell, 2023).

177. A new species of burrowing frog, *Synapturanus danta* has been identified in Peru. The frog has gotten tons of attention because it looks like the famous chocolate frogs in Harry Potter (Greenwell, 2023).

Extinct Species

178. Animals that have gone extinct and then rediscovered years later are known as "Lazarus species" (Nelson, 2009).

179. Did you know that approximately 99% of all species that have ever lived on Earth have gone extinct? This means that the current flora and fauna in the world represent just 1% (Larkin, 2019).

180. The dodo became extinct due to excessive hunting by sailors and the introduction of new mammals such as monkeys, rats, and pigs to the island of Mauritius (Petruzzello, 2019).

181. The largest flightless bird to ever live was the Elephant bird which weighed over 1000 lbs (454 kg). An ostrich weighs about a tenth of that (Larkin, 2019). 182. Between 1889 and 2011, at least 351 species that were thought to be extinct were rediscovered (Scheffers et al., 2011).

183. The Irish elk which is now extinct had the largest antlers ever seen on deer. They measured approximately 13 ft (4 m) (Larkin, 2019).

Chapter4: Brilliant Buildings and Architecture Facts

184. The oldest building that has been found to date is Göbekli Tepe. It's a temple in Turkey that has been dated 9500–8000 BCE (Forestell, 2021).

185. Edinburgh Castle in Scotland is built on an extinct volcanic hill thought to be approximately 350 million years old (Tedesco, 2020).

186. The Tower of London in England has served as a royal palace, prison, zoo, and treasury over its long history (Cartwright, 2019).

a187. Matsumoto Castle in Japan is one of the oldest wooden castles and is nicknamed "Crow Castle" due to its black exterior (Clinton, 2023).

188. The Dolce by Wyndham Hanoi Golden Lake is the world's first gold-plated hotel! Approximately 2,000 lbs (907 kg) of gold was used to decorate the hotel (Chang, 2020).

189. The Kakslauttanen Arctic Resort in Finland features glass igloos, allowing guests to experience the Northern Lights from the comfort of their rooms (Simpson, 2022).

190. The ancient Chinese developed advanced woodworking techniques, including interlocking beams and columns without the use of nails (*Chinese traditional architectural craftsmanship for timber-framed structures*, 2009).

191. The Inca civilization, known for Machu Picchu, employed a technique called "ashlar" in their buildings. They were able to precisely cut stones to fit together without the use of mortar (Láscar, 2010).

191. The ancient Romans used concrete extensively in their constructions. It was made from a mixture of volcanic ash, lime, and water (Dunham, 2023).

192. Roman concrete used in sea walls has been able to endure ocean waves for more than 2,000 years because the seawater interacts with the concrete to form a mineral that strengthens it (Witze, 2017).

193. The Abraj Al Bait Clock Tower in Mecca, Saudi Arabia, is the world's third-tallest building and houses the world's largest clock face. The 1,972 ft (601 m) tower holds the 141 ft (43 m) diameter clock faces (Stamp, 2019).

194. The Edge in Amsterdam, Netherlands, is considered the greenest office building in the world. It uses 70% less energy than other office buildings (Go Construct Team, 2023).

195. The Bahrain World Trade Center has three massive wind turbines integrated into its design, providing a significant portion of its energy needs (Patoway, 2015b).

196. Considered one of the oldest fortified structures, the Walls of Jericho date back to around 8000 BCE and stand 13 ft (4 m) high (Guilmartin, 2020).

197. The Egyptian Imhotep is considered to be the first architect (and physician) ever named. He was responsible for designing the Step Pyramid of Djoser at

Saqqarah (Mikić, 2008).

198. Dubai's Museum of the Future is the most complex building ever built. The building's unconventional shape required the development of new parametric modeling tools and building algorithms (Dudani, 2022).

199. The smallest house ever to be built is just one square meter in size! The One SQM House was built by architect, Van Bo Le-Metnze of Berlin (Gorgan, 2022).

200. The first treehouse ever mentioned was in first-century Rome. The Roman emperor Gaius Caesar, nicknamed Caligula, ordered a dining hall to be built in the trees (Heichelbech, 2022).

201. The world's first invisible building was the Infinity Tower in South Korea. The building uses cameras to project the image of its surroundings (Cripps, 2013).

202. The oldest building that is still functional and in use today is The Pantheon. It has been used as a Roman Catholic Church since the 7th century (Palumbo, 2020).

203. The world's first megacities were New York and Tokyo. They both reached megacity status in the 1950s.

204. Jakarta, the capital of Indonesia, is a megacity of 30 million people that is sinking! It might become the first megacity claimed by climate change (Guest, 2019).

205. Architects in Tokyo are already working on developing an underwater city! They already have the plans in place and it may become a reality by 2030 (Alexander, 2020).

206. Kansai International Airport is the longest hotel in the world and was built on an artificial island in Osaka Bay (Crook, 2019).

207. Industrial-sized 3D printers can print an entire house in just 24 hours (Becher, 2023).

208. The Alcántara Bridge over the Tagus River in Spain was built in 106 CE and is still in use today (Ricketts, 2018).

209. Architecture was once an Olympic sport (De Graaf, 2015).

210. The Bahnhof Data Center in Sweden is one of the most secure buildings in the world. Located 98 ft (30 m) under a granite mountain, this bunker can survive a hydrogen bomb (Cortese, 2019).

211. The Empire State Building contains 10 million bricks (T. Forestell, 2021).

212. The Stone House in Portugal sits between two giant rocks and was inspired by The Flintstones (Cilento, 2010).

213. The Great Wall of China took over 2,000 years to build (Vermeulen, 2021).

Chapter5: Powerful Plant Facts

214. The *Rafflesia arnoldii*, or Corpse Lily, produces the world's largest flower, with a diameter of up to 3 ft (1 m) (Schaefer, 2022).

215. Before trees, *Prototaxites* were tall fungi that grew 3 feet in diameter and around 26 ft (8 m) tall (Stearns, 2020)!

216. For commercial vanilla bean production in countries outside Mexico, each vanilla flower must be pollinated by hand to produce the vanilla bean (Kahane et al., 2008).

217. The record for the world's largest seed goes to the Coco de Mer. The seed measures up to 12 in (30.5 cm) long and weighs over 40 lbs (20 kg) (Richins Myers, 2019).

218. Bamboo is incredibly fast-growing. Some species can grow up to 3 ft (0.91 m) per day (Villazon, 2021).

219. The Titan Arum, also known as the "corpse flower," holds the record for being the world's tallest flowering plant. It can reach heights of over 10 ft (3 m) (Petruzzello, 2018).

220. The corpse flower also stinks and is warm to the touch (Stearns, 2020).

221. The color of hydrangea flowers can change based on soil pH. Acidic soil tends to produce blue flowers, while alkaline soil results in pink flowers (Coulter, 2016).

222. Maple syrup is produced from the sap of sugar maple trees. It takes approximately 40 gallons (150 liters) of sap to produce 1 gallon (3.8 liters) of syrup (Chesman, 2014).

223. Catnip is a much more effective mosquito repellent than commercial insect repellent (Reichert et al., 2019).

224. Some plants release chemicals into the soil through a process called allelopathy, inhibiting the growth of nearby competing plants (Li et al., 2021).

225. Mangrove trees have unique adaptations to thrive in salty coastal environments, including filtering saltwater and excreting excess salt through special glands (Srikanth et al., 2015).

226. Olive trees can live for centuries, and some ancient olive trees are believed to be over 500 years old (Camarero et al., 2021).

227. Some pine trees, like the pitch pine, have serotinous cones that only open and release seeds in response to the heat of a fire (Muether Brown, 2021).

228. Tulip bulbs were once so highly valued in the Netherlands during the 17th century that they were traded as a form of currency in a speculative market as "Tulip Mania" (Roos, 2020).

229. The Wollemi pine, a rare and ancient tree species, was thought to be extinct until its rediscovery in 1994 in a remote part of Australia (Yatskievych, 2020).

230. The roots of the *Ficus elastica*, or rubber tree, are used to grow living bridges that people use in India, Indonesia, and Java (Stearns, 2020).

231. The Elephant grass found in Africa got its name by being the favorite food of elephants! It's now also used for cattle (Kovacevic, 2021).

232. Oak trees are struck by lightning more than any other tree, mostly due to their height (Roark, 2022).

233. It takes about 20 years before an oak tree can start producing acorns (Bingaman, 2011).

234. In 2009, scientists discovered the largest carnivorous plant in the Philippines, capable of devouring rats. *Nepenthes attenboroughii* is a new species of pitcher plant (Fox, 2009).

235. Scientists were able to revive a 32,000-year-old flowering plant from the fossilized fruit found in a stash made by an Ice Age squirrel (Kaufman, 2012).

236. Ghost plants don't need sunlight to survive because they don't photosynthesize. They gain their nutrients from a fungal host (Sullivan, 2021a).

237. A notch in a tree will stay the same distance from the ground as the tree grows (Higgins, 2018).

238. Saffron comes from a type of crocus flower. It costs so much because it has to be harvested by hand and each flower produces a small amount (Grannan, 2019).

239. Different parts of a tree grow at different times throughout the year (Duryea & Malavasi, 2021).

240. There's a palm tree in Madagascar that commits suicide! It grows for approximately 100 years before flowering so profusely that it uses up all its reserves (Candy, 2008).

241. The manchineel tree is one of the most dangerous trees in the world. The sap of the tree and its fruit can burn skin and strip the paint off cars (Strickland, 2000).

242. Another dangerous tree is sandbox tree. When the seeds of the tree are mature, they explode sending the seeds flying at speeds of 150 miles (241 km) per hour (Carroll, 2015).

243. There are 422 trees for every person on Earth (Kilgore, 2022).

244. The world's rarest tree is the Three Kings Kaikomako of New Zealand. There is only a single tree left in the wild (Platt, 2023).

Chapter6: Fascinating Flying Objects

255. Kites were invented in ancient China over 2,000 years ago. They were initially used for military signaling (National Air and Space Museum, 2017).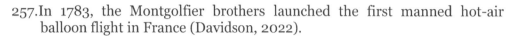

256. 850 BCE marks the first recorded attempt at human flight in New Troy. built a pair of wings that attached to his arms (Fuller, 2008).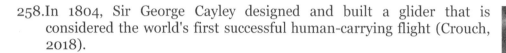

257. In 1783, the Montgolfier brothers launched the first manned hot-air balloon flight in France (Davidson, 2022).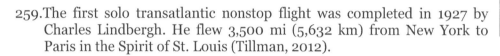

258. In 1804, Sir George Cayley designed and built a glider that is considered the world's first successful human-carrying flight (Crouch, 2018).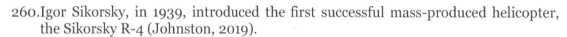

259. The first solo transatlantic nonstop flight was completed in 1927 by Charles Lindbergh. He flew 3,500 mi (5,632 km) from New York to Paris in the Spirit of St. Louis (Tillman, 2012).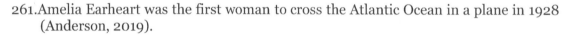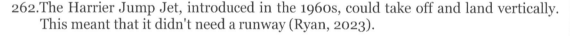

260. Igor Sikorsky, in 1939, introduced the first successful mass-produced helicopter, the Sikorsky R-4 (Johnston, 2019).

261. Amelia Earheart was the first woman to cross the Atlantic Ocean in a plane in 1928 (Anderson, 2019).

262. The Harrier Jump Jet, introduced in the 1960s, could take off and land vertically. This meant that it didn't need a runway (Ryan, 2023).

263. The largest paper airplane ever made had a wingspan of 45 feet and was launched from a height of 2,703 feet in 2012.

264. Jetpack enthusiasts have achieved impressive flights. However, in 2020 many aircraft landing in Los Angeles reported that a man in a jetpack was flying alongside the plane (Stone & Kaji, 2020).

265. Airplanes can get struck by lightning (Locker, 2016).

266. A Boeing 747 is more fuel-efficient than a car and can hold 48,400 gallons of fuel (Crow & Weisman, 2019).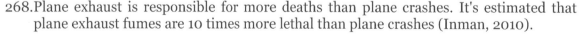

267. Dead chickens are thrown into a plane's jets during safety tests (Crow & Weisman, 2019).

268. Plane exhaust is responsible for more deaths than plane crashes. It's estimated that plane exhaust fumes are 10 times more lethal than plane crashes (Inman, 2010).

269. The world's smallest plane weighs only 358.8 lbs (162.7 kg) and was featured in a James Bond movie (Thompson, 2014).

270. A rooster, a duck, and a sheep were the first passengers in a hot air balloon (Grundhauser, 2018).

271. The air within a hot-air balloon needs to be 248°F (120°C) to be able to lift an adult male. That's hot enough to boil water (Woodford, 2011).

272. Hot air balloons can't fly in the rain (Hubbell, 2021).

273. Hopper or cloud hopper balloons are small, one-man hot air balloons. Instead of a basket, there is either a harness or a single seat into which a person can strapped (Langley, n.d.).

274. Tom Morgan flew 15.5 mi (25 km) and reached 8,000 ft (2,438 m) in a lawn chair attached to 100 colorful helium balloons (Earl, 2017).

275. A man named Michel Lottito ate a Cessna 150! It took him 2 years to consume the plane (Atwal, 2022).

276. The first documented sighting of an unidentified flying object was in 1947 in Mount Rainier, Washington (Shostak, 2019).

277. In 2019 Marcelo Prieto, Rafael Saladini, and Rafael de Moraes Barros covered a distance of 365 mi (588 km) in 11 hours paragliding (Plessis, 2020).

278. The longest straight distance covered by a hang glider was 475 mi (764 km) by Dustin Martin in 2012 (Hurni, 2016).

279. There are tiny drones called Micro Air Vehicles (MAVs) which are used for surveillance and exploration (Coppola et al., 2020).

280. Engineers have taken it one step further and modeled these tiny robots after birds, bats, and insects to make them more stealthy (Baggaley, 2019).

281. December 1945, when not one but six planes vanished over the Bermuda Triangle. Five Avenger torpedo bombers and a passenger plane carrying 13 passengers were never recovered (Anderson, 2019).

282. The first toilet on a plane was installed in 1982. Before that, people had to use a box and pilots were known to relieve themselves in their shoes (Smith, 2022).

283. Goodyear created the Inflatoplane, or GA-33, as a way for stranded soldiers to escape. The plane had to be inflated with a hand pump (Trevithick, 2015).

284. The Vought V-173 was given the name Flying Pancake because of its strange flat, round shape (Wright, 2013).

285. Fun Fact: You can build your own helicopter! The Safari 400 helicopter kit takes just over 500 hours to assemble with only hand tools (Branch, 2020).

Chapter7: Dazzling Dinosaurs

286. The term "dinosaur" was coined by Sir Richard Owen in 1842, combining the Greek words "deinos" (terrible) and "sauros" (lizard) (Osterloff, 2018).

287. The first dinosaur to be named was the megalosaurus in 1824 by Reverend William Buckland (Constantino, 2015).

288. Tyrannosaurus Rex teeth could exceed 12 in (30 cm) in length, and they were serrated like steak knives for tearing flesh (Rafferty, 2023).

289. Many dinosaurs, including velociraptors, had feathers (Rafferty, 2020).

290. Not all dinosaurs were giants. The microraptor was the size of a chicken (Weber, 2019).

291. Fossils of dinosaurs have been discovered in Antarctica (Booth, 1991).

292. The dinosaur with the longest scientific name is *Micropachycephalosaurus* (Mark, 2023).

293. The kosmoceratops was a dinosaur that had 15 horns sticking out of its face (Wighton, 2022).

294. Fossilized dinosaur droppings, known as coprolites, provide valuable information about the diets and digestive systems of dinosaurs (Osterloff & Hendry, 2018).

295. Ichthyornis, a bird-like dinosaur, had teeth in its beak (Dunham, 2018).

296. When the iguanodon was first reconstructed, its thumb was placed on top of its nose(Wighton, 2022).

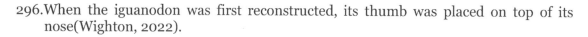

297. Ichnology is the study of trace fossils, including dinosaur footprints, nest sites, and burrows (Gingras, 2021, pp. 669–680).

298. The name "velociraptor" means speedy thief (Lehnardt, 2017).

299. Some dinosaurs swallowed stones (gastroliths) to aid in digestion by grinding food in their stomachs (Rayne, 2021).

300. The biggest dinosaur eggs ever found were about 24 in (61 cm) long (Robinson, 2020).

301. On the flip side, the smallest dinosaur eggs were 1.8 in (4.5 cm)(Senda, 2020).

302. Argentinosaurus reached heights of up to 115 ft (37 m). A single vertebra of this dinosaur was the size of a fully-grown human (Rafferty, 2019a).

303. Most dinosaurs had long tails that helped them to keep their balance when running (Lehnardt, 2017).

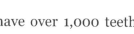

304. A Sauropod called *Patagotitan mayorum* is officially the largest animal to walk the Earth. It weighed approximately 69 tons which is equivalent to 12 African elephants (Montanari, 2017a).

305. The toothiest dinosaur was the hadrosaur. It could have over 1,000 teeth and it continually grew new ones (Eager, 2013).

306. Almost all carnivorous dinosaurs had hollow bones to make them lighter and more agile (Julião, 2023).

307. Paleontologists estimate that 65% of all dinosaurs were herbivores (Okoyomon, 2022).

308. The first recorded description of a possible dinosaur bone discovery dates back to 3,500 years ago in China (Lehnardt, 2017).

309. Dinosaurs have really small brains for such large animals. For example, the *Ampelosaurus* had a brain just slightly larger than a walnut (Black, 2013)

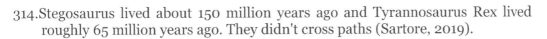

310. The oldest dinosaur fossil is 243 million years old (Holder, 2023b).

311. Dinosaurs died nearly 65 million years before humans evolved on Earth (Scharping, 2023).

312. Nobody knows for certain what color dinosaurs were. Paleontologists think they were very brightly colored just like birds due to fossilized feathers found (Hamer, 2022).

313. Dinosaur skulls had extremely large holes that helped to regulate temperatures inside their head (Starr, 2019).

314. Stegosaurus lived about 150 million years ago and Tyrannosaurus Rex lived roughly 65 million years ago. They didn't cross paths (Sartore, 2019).

315. Dinosaurs had fleas. They measured between 0.3–0.8 in (8–21 mm) in size (Switek, 2012).

316. Most of the world's dinosaur fossils are found in three places: China, Argentina, and North America (Wighton, 2022).

Chapter8: Captivating Car Facts

317. The cheapest car ever made was the Tata Nano (Smith, 2022). This five-seater 4 door car was sold at around $2500 when it came out to the market.

318. Toyota holds the record for the largest number of cars sold by a single company in a single year, with over 10 million cars in 2022 (Reuters, 2023a).

319. Emil and Liliana Schmid hold the record for the longest road trip in the world! The couple has been driving around since 1984 and the total distance covered is 460,476 miles (741,065 km) (Gorgan, 2021). That's almost equal to 18 times the Earth's circumference.

320. The Peel P50 holds the title of the world's smallest production car, measuring only 54 in (137 cm) long and 39 in (99 cm) wide (Khan, 2023).

321. The first car radio was introduced by Chevrolet in 1922, but it wasn't until the 1930s that car radios became more widely available (Holm, 2022).

322. The full-size Chevrolet pickup was the most stolen vehicle in the United States in 2022 (Paulus, 2021).

323. The concept of the airbag was first patented in 1951, but it only became widespread in cars in the 1980s (Bellis, 2018).

324. The first car to feature a GPS navigation system was the 1981 Honda Accord and Honda Vigor vehicles (Berger, 2017).

325. The Rimac Nevera is an electric hypercar with a top speed of 258 mph (415 kph) (O'Kane, 2021).

326. Globally, the most popular car color is white, with approximately 25.8% of cars on the road being white (Gorzelany, 2022).

327. The world's first record of a car rental service is from 1904 in Minneapolis (Salon, 2022).

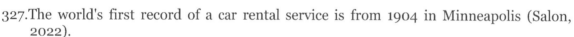

328. The first convertible car was the 1935 Peugeot 402 (DeMichiel, 2023).

329. The first recorded car crash occurred in 1891 in Ohio, involving two steam-powered cars (Tapalaga, 2022).

330. The Land Rover Defender was in production for 68 years from 1948 to 2016 (Pitas, 2016).

331. Rolls-Royce vehicles often come equipped with an umbrella stored in the door frame, a feature introduced in the 1950s (Graham, 2020).

332. It was not until the 1920s that the first widely distributed rearview mirror came out. Elmen Berger called it the "Cop Spotter" because it was to help drivers avoid the police (Cabral, 2023).

333. The title of the world's biggest land vehicle goes to the RWE Bagger 288. It's used for mining operations in Germany (Hawley, 2023). It is approximately 220m long, 46m wide, 96m high, and weighs 13500 tons and has 12 caterpillar tracks! It spins 21m diameter blade to dig the ground.

334.The Porsche 911's distinctive silhouette has remained largely unchanged since its introduction in 1963 (Winfrey, 2014).

335.A woman named Mary Anderson invented windshield wipers in 1902 (Palca, 2017).

336.Ferrari only manufactures about 9,000 cars a year (Jones, 2019).

337.The world's largest car collection belongs to the Sultan of Brunei Darussalam. He has over 7,000 cars (Pellegrino, 2023).

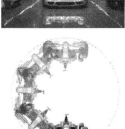

338.95% of a car's lifetime is spent parked (Morris, 2016).

339.A modern Formula 1 car can potentially drive upside down in a tunnel at 120mph (193 kph). The cars generate enough downforce at high speeds to be able to stick to the surface (Mitchell, 2013).

340.In 2022, 85 million cars were produced globally. This amounts to 23,288 cars made every day (Placek, 2023).

341.The record for the world's fastest wheel change on a moving car belongs to Manuel Zoldan and Gianluca Folco. They set the record of 1 minute 17 seconds (Edelstein, 2022).

342.Dubai policemen sport the fastest police cars. The Bugatti Veyron's top speed is 253 mph (407 kph) (Scott, 2017).

343.The first cars were operated by a crank and did not have steering wheels (Williams, 2020).

344.The average weight of a car in 2022 was 4,094 pounds (1857 kg) (Hawley, 2022).

345.The highest number of people to fit in a car is 20. An entire cheerleading squad fitted into a Smart Car (Molnar, 2019).

346.The Plymouth Voyager and Dodge Caravan are credited as the world's first minivans (Zhang, 2017).

347.In 1964, the president of Mexico, Adolfo Mateos, ran his car on tequila (Lehto, 2017).

Chapter9: Riveting Rivers, Lakes and Waterfalls

348. At 4,000 mi (6,400 km), the length of the Amazon River is equivalent to the distance from New York City to Rome (Parsons et al., 2018).

349. The Volga River in Europe is the longest river in Europe (García de Durango, 2019).

350. During the dry season, water flows from the Tonle Sap Lake in Southeast Asia into the Mekong River. In the wet season, it changes so that water flowers from the river to the lake (Oeurng et al., 2019).

351. The Colorado River carved out the Grand Canyon over millions of years (Witze, 2019).

352. The Great Lakes—Superior, Michigan, Huron, Erie, and Ontario—contain about 84% of North America's fresh surface water (Environmental Protection Agency, 2019).

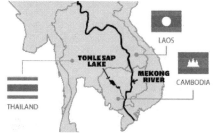

353. Glacial lakes, such as those in the Himalayas, are formed by the melting of glaciers (Fitzsimons & Howarth, 2018, pp. 309–334).

354. Lake Maracaibo in Venezuela experiences the Catatumbo lightning phenomenon, where lightning occurs almost every day (Martinez, 2022).

355. Iguazu Falls, on the border of Argentina and Brazil, is a system of 275 waterfalls (The Editors of Encyclopedia Britannica, 2019).

356. The Plitvice Lakes in Croatia feature a series of cascading waterfalls connecting 16 lakes (Mat, 2023d).

357. Lake Nyos Disaster in Cameroon in 1986 resulted in the release of a deadly cloud of carbon dioxide that led to the sudden suffocation of people and animals in the surrounding area (Backhouse, 2022).

Chapter10: Magnificent Mountains and Volcanoes

358. The Andes mountain range in South America is the longest continental mountain range, stretching over 5,500 mi (8,900 km) (Stewart et al., 2017).

359. Mount Elbrus in Russia, the highest peak in Europe is 18,510 ft (5,642 m) high. It's also a dormant volcano (Jhingan, 2020).

360. The Barberton Greenstone Belt between South Africa and Swaziland is considered one of the oldest mountains in the world, formed over 3.6 billion years ago (Agard, 2023).

361. The phenomenon known as the "Brocken Spectre" occurs when a person's shadow is cast upon clouds or mist in front of them (Byrd, 2019).

362. The Caucasus Mountains were crossed by ancient trade routes, connecting Europe and Asia. Large caravans of people and animals would travel the route (Elliott, 2022).

363. Mount Vesuvius, near Naples, Italy, famously erupted in 79 CE, burying the cities of Pompeii and Herculaneum (Bileta, 2023).

364. The eruption of Krakatoa occurred in Indonesia in 1883 was one of the most powerful in recorded history, causing global climate effects (Kiger, 2020).

365. Submarine volcanoes are common features on the ocean floor, contributing to the formation of underwater mountain ranges (Portillo, 2023).

366. Many islands, like Hawaii and Iceland, are volcanic in origin and have central shield volcanoes (Takahashi, 2010).

367. The word "volcano" is derived from Vulcan, the Roman god of fire.

Chapter11: Remarkable Rainforests

368. The Daintree Rainforest in Australia is believed to be the oldest rainforest in the world, dating back over 135 million years (Holder, 2023a).

369. The average temperature of the tropical rainforest remains between 68 and 84°F (20 and 29°C) (Smith, 2018).

370. The Amazon holds more species of flora and fauna than any other terrestrial ecosystem on the planet (Butler, 2020).

371. Some fungi in the lesser-known Atlantic Forest in Brazil are bioluminescent, creating an otherworldly glow in the dark (Rellihan, 2023).

372. Some palm trees in the rainforests of Latin America are known as "walking palm trees." They slowly move towards better sunlight by growing their roots in the direction they want to go (Gaeng, 2023a).

373. The loss of rainforests often leads to drought. Rainforests add water to the atmosphere through the process of transpiration and fewer trees means less water in the atmosphere (MacDonald, 2018).

374. The warm and humid conditions of rainforests lead to rapid decomposition of dead organic matter, with fallen leaves often decomposing within weeks (Ruiz, 2020).

375. Two different types of rainforests exist: temperate and tropical (Cranham, 2019).

376. Trees in tropical rainforests are so dense that it takes approximately 10 minutes for a raindrop to reach the ground from the canopy (National Geographic, 2023b).

377. Rainforests make up 6% of land on Earth. In 1947, their coverage was 14% (National Geographic, 2023b).

Chapter 12: Dauntless Deserts

378. The Dry Valleys in Antarctica are considered the driest places on Earth. It has not rained there for two million years (Cain, 2008a).

379. The largest sand dune in the world is in Argentina. Duna Federico Kirbus measures 4,035 ft (1,230 m) high (Feniou, 2023).

380. Badwater Basin in Death Valley, USA, is the lowest point in North America, lying 282 feet (86 meters) below sea level (Yu, 2023).

381. The desert pupfish, found in the Mojave Desert, has adapted to survive in extremely saline water, even tolerating water temperatures above 90°F (32°C) (Miller, 2014).

382. The Khongoryn Els sand dunes in the Gobi Desert are known as Duut Mankhan or "singing dunes" because of the sound they make when the sand is disturbed (Brooks, 2021).

383. "Desert roses" are crystalline formations found in arid regions, often composed of minerals like gypsum or barite (Hope et al., 2015).

384. Dasht-e Kavir in Iran is a massive salt desert. It's dangerous to travel through this desert as some of the areas have quicksand-like properties (Patowary, 2015a).

385. Some deserts, like the Yucatan Desert in Mexico, have cenotes—natural sinkholes filled with groundwater (Ryoo, 2021).

386. Wadi Rum in Jordan is also known as the Valley of the Moon or Mars on Earth due to the color of its dunes (Jolly, 2023).

387. The sand in Wadi Rum gets its distinctive red color from iron oxide (Jolly, 2023).

388. Furnace Creek Ranch in Death Valley, USA, recorded one of the highest temperatures on Earth at 134°F (56.7°C) in 1913 (Erdman, 2023).

389. The Atacama Desert in Chile which is one of the driest places on Earth experiences a colorful desert bloom after receiving rain (Bonaccorso, 2022).

390. The residents of the Atacama Desert use fog nets to harvest water from coastal fog (Milesi, 2020).

391. Desert mirages, such as the Fata Morgana, create optical illusions due to temperature inversions in the air (Lew, 2017).

392. In 2022, the deserts of Saudi Arabia experienced hailstorms, carpeting the desert in white (Elkallawy, 2022).

393. The Saharan Desert once had a vast river network beneath the surface that provided crucial water sources for plants and animals (Sample, 2015).

394. Salar de Atacama in Chile's Atacama Desert holds significant lithium

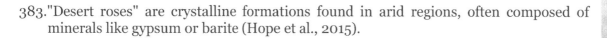

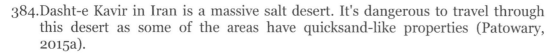

reserves, a key element in batteries for electric vehicles (Villegas, 2023).

395. The Atacama Rover Astrobiology Drilling Studies, or ARADS team tests tools and techniques in the Atacama Desert. The desert's arid conditions make it an ideal location due to its similarity to Mars (Tabor, 2019).

396. The largest oasis in the world is the Al-Hasa oasis, also known as the Al-Ahsa oasis, located in eastern Saudi Arabia. It is an expansive oasis region covering approximately 85.4 km² (33 sq mi) and is renowned for its abundant palm groves, fertile agricultural land, and natural springs.

397. One-third of the Earth's surface is barren land or desert land (Cain, 2010).

398. Every year, approximately 46,000 square miles (120,000 square kilometers) are turned into actual deserts (The World Counts, 2023). That's approximately equivalent to the size of 23 million standard football stadiums.

399. The Sahara desert is 10% larger now than it was in 1920. Scientists believe that this rate of expansion is due to climate change (Weisberger, 2018).

400. The Aralkum Desert is the newest formed desert on record. It appeared in 1960 in what was once the Aral Sea between Uzbekistan and Kazakhstan (Dempsey, 2014).

401. Almost 1,000 square miles (2,590 square kilometers) of Chinese land turns into deserts each year (Funnell, 2019).

402. The Marathon Des Sables is one of the most extreme ultramarathons on Earth. It involves a 155 mi (250 km) trek through the Sahara, over a period of 7 days (Hobson, 2019).

403. On February 18th, 1979, snow fell in the Sahara for the first time (Daley, 2016).

404. Sandstorms in the desert create friction between sand particles that generate static electricity. This leads to the development of electric fields in the air (Choi, 2010). So when your hairs stand up in the middle of the desert, watch out, thunders coming!

405. The Ica Desert in Peru is home to the mysterious Nazca Lines, ancient geoglyphs etched into the desert floor (Tharpe, 2023).

406. The rain shadow effect is when mountains block rainfall and create deserts. Death Valley formed as a result of the rain shadow effect from the Sierra Nevada mountain range (Means, 2021).

407. The creosote bush, found in the Chihuahuan and Mojave Deserts, is one of the oldest living plants. The oldest is estimated to be 11,700 years old (Schalau, 2021).

408. Deserts often offer exceptionally clear and dark skies, providing stunning views of stars and celestial phenomena (Busqué, 2023).

Chapter13: Delightful DNA Facts

409. The human genome consists of approximately 3 billion base pairs of DNA (National Human Genome Research Institute, 2023b).

410. The oldest DNA found, extracted, and analyzed by scientists was two million years old. They were plant and animal DNA fragments found in Greenland (Pappas, 2022).

411. Synthetic biologists engineer DNA to create artificial organisms for various purposes by combining biological systems and technology (Garner, 2021).

412. NASA once conducted a study comparing the DNA of astronaut Scott Kelly with his twin brother Mark. The "Twins Study" showed that Scott's gene expression was different in space (NASA, 2019).

413. Artists and scientists have encoded DNA sequences into musical compositions (Temple, 2017).

414. DNA is used in conservation efforts to preserve the genetic diversity of endangered species (Greenwood, 2021).

415. Teeth are particularly well-preserved over time, making them valuable sources of DNA for archaeological studies (Forshaw, 2022).

416. Harvard researchers used sequencing technology to store 70 billion copies of a book in DNA binary code (Mearian, 2012).

417. In 2012, it was estimated that the entire world's information at the time–1.8 zettabytes–could be stored in about 4 grams of DNA (Mearian, 2012). Digital information is traditionally stored in binary form, using a sequence of 0s and 1s to represent all types of data. DNA storage transcends binary by utilizing its four-character code (adenine [A], thymine [T], guanine [G], and cytosine [C]) to encode information. This quadruple coding system significantly increases storage density, allowing DNA to store data more compactly than binary-based storage devices. Essentially, DNA can hold more information in a smaller physical space because each nucleotide (A, T, G, C) can represent twice as much information as a binary digit (0 or 1), making DNA an incredibly efficient medium for data storage.

418. The size range of human chromosomes is about 50 million to 300 million base pairs (National Human Genome Research Institute, 2023a).

419. You can get animal DNA out of thin air! Scientists were able to collect DNA from the air around the Hamerton Zoo Park (Hoyt, 1970).

420. Less than 2% of our DNA is genes (Cox, 2023).

421. The 98% non-gene portion of our DNA used to be called "junk DNA" or "dark DNA" because of how little it was understood (Cox, 2023).

422. A cell divides approximately two trillion times a day! Every time it divides, a complete copy of our DNA, which is three billion digits long, has to occur (King Abdullah University of Science and Technology, 2018).

423. DNA can be damaged by radiation and chemicals (Ward et al., 1987).

424.DNA modification is a process by which deliberate lab-based changes are made to the DNA sequence (M. Smith, 2022). A recent example is salmons that were modified so that they grow to desirable edible size in 18 months instead of normal 3 years.

425.You share 98.7% of your DNA in common with chimpanzees and bonobos (Yong, 2023).

426. 25 April is celebrated annually as National DNA Day in the United States holiday (National Human Genome Research Institute, 2023a).

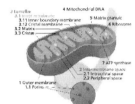

427.Although each cell contains a full complement of DNA, each cell uses genes selectively depending on the function required (Genetic Alliance, 2009).

428.Genetic factors don't just determine how you look; they also influence behavior (Baker, 2007).

429.Y-chromosomal DNA is used for tracing paternal ancestry since It's passed from father to son (McDermott, 2019).

430.Similarly, your mitochondrial DNA is inherited solely from your mother, making it useful for tracing maternal ancestry (National Human Genome Research Institute, 2013). Mitochondria are like tiny power plants in cells, making energy (ATP) for the body to stay healthy and active.

431.Gene therapy involves altering genes to treat or prevent genetic diseases (Landhuis, 2021).

432.DNA vaccines involve introducing DNA-encoding antigens into the body to stimulate an immune response (Leitner et al., 1999).

433.DNA nanobots are tiny, programmable structures made of DNA strands that can perform specific tasks. They are being researched to target cancer cells (Singh & Deshmukh, 2022).

434.No one else on Earth has the same DNA as you! Unless you have an identical twin (Smith-Garcia, 2021).

435.Viruses use either DNA or RNA to infect organisms (Segre, 2023).

436.Sir Alec Jeffreys developed the technique of DNA fingerprinting in 1984, revolutionizing forensic science and paternity testing (McKie, 2017).

437.The Combined DNA Index System (CODIS) is a national DNA database in the United States used to store and match DNA profiles from criminal cases Norrgard, 2008).

438.Conditions like cystic fibrosis and sickle cell anemia are caused by specific single-gene mutations (Clancy, 2008).

439.Cells have intricate mechanisms to repair damaged DNA, helping maintain the integrity of the genetic code (Cooper, 2000).

Chapter14: Fabulous Fishery Facts

440. Commercial crab fishing is one of the most dangerous occupations due to the rough seas and equipment used (Jacobs, 2021).

441. As of 2020, the number of people fishing and practicing aquaculture worldwide amounts to almost 59 million (Shahbandeh, 2022).

442. The longest fishing rod measures 73 ft 7 in (22 m 45 cm) and was created by Schweizerischer Fischereiverband (Guinness World Records, 2011).

443. Aquaculture, or fish farming, is the fastest-growing sector in food production, providing more than half of the world's seafood (Ritchie, 2019).

444. Aquaculture practiced in marine environments is called mariculture. Fish are reared and harvested from pens in their natural environments (Phillips, 2009).

445. In 2021, the average American consumed a record 20.5 lbs (9.3 kg) of seafood (Chase, 2023).

446. Fisheries often impose size limits to allow fish to reach maturity and reproduce before being caught (Lavin et al., 2021).

447. Approximately 33.1% of global fish stocks are overfished, meaning they are harvested faster than they can reproduce (Ritchie & Roser, 2021).

448. The international trade in fish and fishery products is valued at over $151 billion annually (Food and Agriculture Organization, 2022).

449. The demand for fish with high omega-3 content has driven market trends, leading to increased production of species like salmon (Troell et al., n.d.).

450. One of the farthest surfcasting ever was achieved by Danny Moeskops of Belgium in 2018. Moeskops casted a fishing line an astounding distance of 286.22 meters (938 feet 10 inches).

451. About 38.5 million tons of bycatch results from deep sea trawling each year (Wong, 2020).

452. Marine Protected Areas (MPAs) are designated zones where fishing is restricted or prohibited to protect marine ecosystems and promote biodiversity (Kriegl et al., 2021).

453. Abandoned or lost fishing gear, known as ghost gear, continues to catch and kill marine life, contributing to environmental issues (Giskes, 2022).

454. Climate change affects fisheries by altering ocean temperatures, currents, and the distribution of fish species (Serpetti et al., 2017).

455. The biggest recorded tuna to date was an Atlantic bluefin captured near Nova Scotia, weighing 1,496 pounds.(678kg).

456. Aquaponics combines aquaculture and hydroponics, allowing the simultaneous cultivation of fish and plants in a symbiotic environment (Hoering, 2021).

457. Fishing quotas are in place globally to set limits on the amount of fish that can be caught in the wild

(Hall, 2021).

458. Sturgeon fisheries produce caviar, a luxury food item with high market value. It's estimated that sturgeon fisheries produce 260 tons of caviar annually (Bronzi & Rosenthal, 2014).

459. Approximately 20 percent of fish come from illegal fisheries or from illegal, unreported, and unregulated (IUU) fishing (Collyns, 2022).

460. It's estimated that fishers remove more than 170 billion lbs (77 billion kg) of wildlife from the sea each year (National Geographic, 2023a). That is roughly the same as 14 million elephants!

461. Global fish and seafood production has quadrupled over the past 50 years (Ritchie & Roser, 2023).

462. Half a century ago, the average person ate half as much seafood as we do now (Ritchie, 2019).

463. Aquaculture has an annual growth rate of 8.8% as compared to 2.8% for terrestrial meat production (Karisa, 2023).

464. Thailand, which has one of the biggest aquaculture industries, lost almost half its mangrove forests due to shrimp farming (Ratcliffe & Siradapuvadol, 2023).

465. In 2022, 89% of fish produced in fisheries were consumed by humans, the rest are used for non-food purposes such as fishmeal and fish oil (FAO, 2022).

466. Peru is home to the world's biggest fishery. They farm anchovies(Poortvliet, 2019).

467. Anglers spend more than $1 billion a year on bait alone (Clay, 2014).

468. After World War II, traditional handmade nets made of natural fiber were replaced with more complex, synthetic fiber. The new nets were more durable and could hold more fish (Agarwal, 2022).

469. Fishing is one of the most dangerous jobs in the United States. Fishing and hunting have the highest occupational fatality rate at 132.1 fatal injuries per 100,000 workers in 2020 (Hoff, 2021).

470. Fish and fish products are the most traded food products globally (Wilen, 2023).

Chapter15: Outstanding Ocean and Island Facts

471. The Challenger Deep in the Mariana Trench is the deepest known point in the world's oceans, reaching a depth of about 36,000 ft (11,000 m) (Wattles & McDonald, 2023).

472. Large areas of the ocean are considered "ocean deserts" due to low oxygen and nutrient levels (Renfrow, 2009).

473. Large systems of rotating ocean currents are called ocean gyres. They are a result of the Earth's rotation and global wind patterns (Rafferty, 2009).

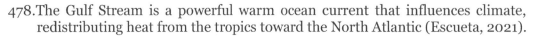
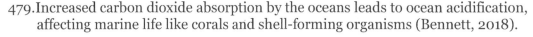
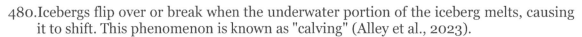

474. The largest waterfall on Earth is underwater and is called the Denmark Strait. The cold water from the surface is pulled down creating a flow of water over 2 mi (3.2 km) deep (Griffith, 2021).

475. Blue holes are underwater sinkholes. The Great Blue Hole off the coast of Belize, Central America extends 410 ft (125 m) into the Earth's crust (Wilkin & Cameron, 2019).

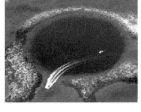

478. The Gulf Stream is a powerful warm ocean current that influences climate, redistributing heat from the tropics toward the North Atlantic (Escueta, 2021).

479. Increased carbon dioxide absorption by the oceans leads to ocean acidification, affecting marine life like corals and shell-forming organisms (Bennett, 2018).

480. Icebergs flip over or break when the underwater portion of the iceberg melts, causing it to shift. This phenomenon is known as "calving" (Alley et al., 2023).

481. The "marine snow" phenomenon involves the sinking of organic particles from the upper ocean layers to the deep sea, resembling underwater snowfall (Silver, 2015).

482. The White Shark Café is a mysterious area in the Pacific Ocean where great white sharks gather (Emerson, 2018).

483. A single drop of seawater can contain millions of bacterial cells (Raina, 2018).

484. Submarine canyons, like the Monterey Canyon off the coast of California, rival the Grand Canyon in size. Monterey Canyon is approximately 300 mi (470 km) in length (Oard, 2019).

485. Red tides, caused by the rapid proliferation of harmful algae, can lead to the discoloration of ocean waters and negatively impact marine life (Howard, 2019).

486. The Great Pacific Garbage Patch exists because ocean currents transport all litter (Lebreton, 2018).

487. It's estimated that more than eight million tons of plastic enter the oceans every year (Ellis, 2021).

488. Researchers recently discovered there's a massive ocean hidden under the Earth's crust (Fletcher, 2023).

489. Islands are classified as either continental or oceanic. Oceanic islands, like the Galápagos, formed from volcanic activity (Wallace, 1887).

490. Zealandia is a submerged microcontinent almost entirely underwater, with only a small portion, including New Zealand, protruding above the ocean surface (Gorvett, 2023).

491. Due to volcanic activity in October 2023, a newly formed island has been spotted by NASA off the coast of Japan (Lea, 2023).

492. The Uros Islands on Lake Titicaca, are artificially made by floating reed platforms anchored to the lakebed (Eberlien, 2023).

493. Pumice rafts, floating masses of volcanic rock, can travel across oceans, carrying marine life and providing a method of dispersal (Bryan et al., 2012).

494. There are two islands called Big Diomede and Little Diomede that are just 3 mi (4.8 km) apart in distance. However, they are almost 21 hours apart in terms of time (Wood, 2022).

495. Humans have created artificial islands for various purposes, including agriculture and tourism. An example of this would be the Palm Islands of Dubai which have been built to resemble palm trees (Fakharany, 2023).

496. Barrier islands, like those along the Atlantic and Gulf coasts of the United States, provide protection to mainland coasts from storms and erosion (Linhoss, 2018).

497. Atolls, like those found in the Pacific, are raised coral islands (Woodroffe & Biribo, 2011).

498. Easter Island is famous for megalithic structures called Moai (Blumberg, 2008).

499. Due to limited freshwater resources, some islands invest in desalination plants to convert seawater into potable water for residents (Derler, 2019).

500. Despite rising sea levels some reef islands in the Pacific are growing in size (Warne, 2015).

501. Hashima Island, also known as Battleship Island because of its shape, has been uninhabited since 1974 (Wenyu, 2017). 502. Hashima Island was used to house the laborers who mined coal on the island. At one stage there was a staggering 5,267 people on the 525 ft by 1,575 ft (160 m by 480 m) island (Wenyu, 2017).

503. All Olympic curling stones are made from a rare type of granite that is only found on Ailsa Craig, a tiny island in Scotland (Fox, 2018).

Chapter16: Marvelous Money Facts

504. The 1933 Double Eagle, a $20 gold coin, holds the record as the most expensive coin ever sold at auction, fetching over $18 million (Holland, 2021).

505. The largest bank heist is the Central Bank of Iraq in Baghdad which was robbed of approximately $920 million in cash (Campbell, 2023).

506. The word "salary" comes from the Latin word "salarium," meaning salt. Roman soldiers were often paid in salt due to its high value (Hordijk, 2014).

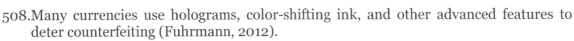

507. The word "money" is derived from the Latin word "moneta," which was taken from the name of the Roman goddess Juno (Saha, n.d.).

508. Many currencies use holograms, color-shifting ink, and other advanced features to deter counterfeiting (Fuhrmann, 2012).

509. Malaysia has the largest banknote in the world measuring 8.7 in x 14.6 in (22 cm x 37 cm)

510. A dollar bill can be folded approximately 4,000 times in its lifetime before it tears (Lovitch, 2022).

511. It costs more to make a penny than it is worth. One penny costs 2.1 cents to produce (Lovitch, 2022).

512. The average lifespan of a banknote is 4 and 10 years for low and high-denomination notes, respectively.

513. Some historical coins had holes in the center, allowing them to be easily carried on a string.

514. Countries like Australia have introduced polymer banknotes that are more durable and waterproof.

515. The Croatian mint produced the world's smallest coin, measuring only 0.07 inches (0.19 centimeters) in diameter (Staff, 2022).

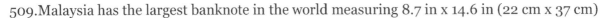

516. Canada has experimented with transparent banknotes made from a polymer substrate.

517. On 22 May 2010, a programmer paid 10,000 bitcoins for two pizzas, marking the first real-world transaction using cryptocurrency (Hankin, 2019).

518. Zimbabwe experienced hyperinflation in the late 2000s, leading to the issuance of a one hundred trillion dollar note (Frisby, 2016).

519. People carved intricate designs on nickels, known as "hobo nickels," as a form of folk art and sometimes as a way to modify the coin's value (McCormick, 2020).

520. In 2007, thieves stole a Canadian gold coin weighing 220 lbs (99.7 kg) and worth over $1 million from the Bode Museum in Berlin. Although arrested, the coin was never recovered (Davis, 2020).

521. In 2021, a woman named Nusrat Jahan Nipa set the Guinness World Record for the tallest stack of coins. She stacked 71 coins in 1 minute (Swapan, 2021).

522. The coin toss originated in ancient Rome and was originally called "Heads or Ships" (Wilde, 2020).

523. Some people put a silver coin in their Christmas pudding mix. Whoever finds it in their slice of pudding is said to have good luck in the new year (Groome, 2016).

524. During a shortage of copper during World War II, the U.S. Mint produced steel pennies in 1943 (The National World War II Museum, 2020).

525. For the 80th anniversary of Monopoly, Hasbro released 80 sets with real money (Peterson, 2015)!

526. The hundred-dollar bill is the most counterfeited banknote globally (Thompson, 2016).

527. In medieval England, tally sticks were used as a form of money. The sticks were marked and then split in half, with each party keeping one part as a record of the transaction (Harford, 2017).

528. The world's oldest bank is in Italy. Banca Monte dei Paschi di Siena was founded in 1472.

529. The Maria Theresa Thaler, a silver coin first minted in 1740, remained a widely accepted trade coin for centuries and is still produced today (Linsboth, n.d.).

530. In colonial America, tobacco served as a de facto currency, and prices were often quoted in pounds of tobacco (Murphy, 2017).

531. Minting errors can make certain coins valuable to collectors. Examples include double strikes, off-center strikes, and missing or misprinted features. One of the most famous sales occurred in January 2010, when one of the five coins of erroneously minted 1913 Liberty Head nickel was sold in a private sale to a collector for a reported $3,737,500.

532. Mansa Musa, the ruler of the Mali Empire in the 14th century, is often considered the richest person in history, with an estimated wealth of $400 billion (Mulroy, 2022b).

533. The slang term "buck" for dollars has uncertain origins, but it may be traced back to when deer skins (bucks) were used as a form of currency in colonial America (Kenton, 2003).

534. There is currently $8.28 trillion in circulation globally (Jeffries, 2023).

Chapter17: Wondrous Weather Facts

535. In 2017, the city of Bandar Mahshahr in Iran recorded one of the highest heat indices ever reported, reaching 165°F (74°C) (Stewart, 2017).

536. The Earth experiences over eight million lightning strikes every day (McCarthy, 2014).

537. Hurricane Patricia, which struck Mexico in 2015, became the strongest hurricane ever recorded in the Western Hemisphere with sustained winds of 215 mph (345 km/h) (Belles, 2018).

538. In 2016, Melbourne, Australia experienced a rare phenomenon called thunderstorm asthma. A large number of people developed respiratory issues during a severe thunderstorm due to the amount of allergens in the air (Thien et al., 2018).

539. Tornadoes that form over water are called waterspouts. They can be as dangerous as their land-based counterparts (Ahmed, 2019).

540. Mawsynram, a village in India, holds the record for the highest average annual rainfall, receiving around 472 in (12,000 mm) per year (Lloyd, 2020).

541. Fire tornadoes can occur during intense wildfires, creating swirling columns of flames and smoke. It can have winds as high as 140 mph (225 kph) and temperatures up to 2,700°F (1482°C) (Gray & Richardson, 2023).

542. St. Elmo's Fire is a weather phenomenon where a visible blue or violet glow appears near pointed objects, such as ship masts, during thunderstorms (Carpineti, 2022).

543. Microbursts are powerful, localized columns of sinking air during a thunderstorm that can reach up to 100 mph and can cause significant damage (Dean, 2021).

544. The eruption of Mount Tambora in 1815 led to the "Year Without a Summer" in 1816, causing widespread crop failures and food shortages (Strickland, 2019).

545. Thundersnow is a rare phenomenon where thunder and lightning occur during a snowstorm, creating a wintry version of a thunderstorm. They are seen mostly in the Colorado Front Range, the upper Great Plains, and the Great Lakes (McKeever, 2023).

546. Dry lightning refers to lightning strikes that occur in the absence of significant rainfall, increasing the risk of wildfires (Branom, 2022).

547. Cryoseism, or frost quakes, occurs when water in the ground quickly freezes and expands until the built-up stress needs to be released (Prociv, 2023).

548. The "Perfect Storm" of 1991 was a rare and powerful combination of a storm and a hurricane that created a destructive storm system in New England (Erdman, 2021).

549. Heat bursts are sudden, intense increases in temperature accompanied by strong winds, sometimes occurring at night and leading to rapid evaporation of moisture (Sistek, 2021).

550. Some of the most intense heart bursts in history include a temperature rise from 100°F(38℃) to 158°F(70℃) in two minutes near Lisbon, Portugal, on July 6, 1949, and 188°F(87℃) temperature recorded in Abadan, Iran in June 1967 (Burt, 2013).

551. Haboobs are intense dust storms that form in arid regions and can reduce visibility to near zero. They can extend 10,000 ft (3,048 m) vertically and be about a mile (1.6 kilometer) wide (Walker-Journey, 2022).

552. Grand Banks, an area just off from Newfoundland is considered the foggiest place on Earth. It's foggy for approximately 200 days a year (Met Office, 2019).

553. The windiest place on the planet is Commonwealth Bay in Antarctica. The average annual windspeed is 50 mph (80.5 kph)but it's not uncommon to experience winds over 150 mph (241 kph) (Sexton, 2017).

554. However, Barrow Island in Western Australia recorded the highest wind gust speed of 253 mph (407 kph) on 10 April 1996 (Erdman & Dolce, 2018).

555. Rain doesn't look like a teardrop when it falls. It's more like a sphere or hamburger bun depending on its size (Helmenstine, 2018).

BARROW ISLAND

556. Sometimes, waterspouts or tornadoes pick up animals and carry them long distances, leading to accounts of frogs or fish falling from the sky (Machholz et al., 2022).

557. The US experiences 75% of the world's tornadoes (Skilling, 2021).

558. The air located around a lightning bolt is heated to around 54,000°F (30,000°C). That's five times hotter than the surface of the sun (NOAA SciJinks, n.d.).

559. Babylonians were the first to predict the weather in 650 B.C. using cloud patterns and the stars (Ambrose, 2021).

560. When the pressure drops 24 millibars in 24 hours, a bomb cyclone occurs. Normal air pressure is around 1 bar, so a bomb cyclone results in an air pressure of around 0.025 bar (Earl, 2022).

561. In Utah, there's pink snow. Sometimes called watermelon snow, the pink hue

is caused by a bacteria called *Chlamydomonas nivalis* (O'Kane, 2023).

562. Blood rain occurs when large amounts of red dust particles are present in the air. Usually, large storms collect dust from the Sahara which is transported to Europe (Cunningham, 2022).

563. A heatwave can make train tracks bend! Since steel expands when it's hot, the tracks can bend with use which is why trains may be canceled (Temperton, 2015).

564. Heatwaves are known to turn grapes into raisins before they are picked from the vine (Maier, 2017).

565. It was so cold in 1684, that the River Thames froze solid for 2 months. It was known as the Great Frost (Srigley, 1960).

566. Over the past 50 years, climate change and extreme weather have resulted in a drastic increase in natural disasters (United Nations, 2021).

Chapter18: Tremendous Technologies

567. ENIAC (Electronic Numerical Integrator and Computer) was primarily developed for military purposes during World War II, particularly for calculating artillery firing tables.

568. But ENIAC was enormous by modern standards, occupying a large room with dimensions of about 8.5 feet by 3 feet by 80 feet and weighing around 30 tons, much larger and heavier that today's desktop computers.

569. Douglas Engelbart invented the computer mouse in 1964 (Hall, 2019).

570. The first computer virus, named Creeper, was created in the early 1970s as an experiment to test cybersecurity (Bales, 2021b).

571. QR codes were invented in 1994 by Masahiro Hara and his team at Denso Wave to track automotive parts (McCurry, 2020).

572. The QR in "QR code" stands for quick response (McCurry, 2020).

573. Martin Cooper, an engineer at Motorola, made the first handheld mobile phone call on April 3, 1973. The DynaTAC 8000X was a whopping 2.4 lbs (1.1 kg) (Korn, 2023).

574. Bluetooth technology, enabling wireless communication between devices, was named after a 10th-century Danish king, Harald "Bluetooth" Gormsson. He is known for bringing the tribes of Denmark together much like how Bluetooth connects different devices and industries (Martindale & Martin, 2019).

575. The first version of a self-driving car was first tested in New York in 1925! Francis Houdina attached a radio control system to a car, controlling it with a remote control (Gautam, 2019).

576. Online shopping increased by 270% between 2014 and 2021 (Hancock, 2022).

577. There are over five billion users of the internet across the globe (Van Gelder, 2023).

578. There is a cyber attack every 39 seconds (Wetzig, 2022).

579. Approximately 95% of all online data breaches happen as a result of human error (Wetzig, 2022).

580. The cost associated with a data breach in a company in the United States amounts to $3.86 million (Abshire, 2021).

581. There are more drone pilots than traditional pilots in the United States Air Force (Watters, 2023).

582. Drone racing has become a sport whereby drone pilots have to navigate complex obstacle courses (Mohmad, 2023).

583. Amazon is considering drone delivery services for packages and goods due to its efficiency (Lewis, 2017).

584. The first robot built was in the 1930s. Its name was Elecktro and was capable of 26 routines and knew 700 words (Bales, 2021a).

585. Japan uses about half a million industrial robots (Bryan, 2019).

586. Speaking of Japan, they have the world's fastest internet speed of 319 terabits per second (Siu, 2022).

587. Worldwide, approximately 40 million tons of electronic waste is generated (*Electronic waste facts,* 2023).

588. There are one billion phones and 300 million laptops produced every year (The World Counts, 2023).

589. Current estimates show that there are about 300 million smart homes in the world. Smart homes have all the devices and appliances linked via an internet connection (Curls, 2023).

590. The Noor Complex solar power farm is the world's largest solar farm and can supply electricity to one million people (Lai, 2022). The size of the farm is almost 7 times Central Park in New York City, or roughly 230 standard football stadiums.

591. The average person spends 145 minutes on social media daily (Wong, 2023).

592. Scientists have created nanobots that are so small that they can enter our bloodstream (Marr, 2023).

593. Neuromorphic computing refers to new technology being developed to mimic the human brain (Glover, 2023).

594. Ralph Lauren has a Polo Tech shirt that monitors your heart rate and breathing during exercise (Smith, 2016).

595. The average American household has over ten connected devices (Rafiq, 2023).

596. In agriculture, robotic arms with sensors are able to accurately harvest plants, and automated vehicles are used to prepare fields for planting (Jones, 2023).

597. Scary fact: A typical internet user will spend approximately 43% of their lives online (Georgiev, 2022).

Chapter19: Popular Places

598. Socotra, Yemen is an archipelago known for its otherworldly landscapes and unique plant species, including the iconic Dragon's Blood Tree (Crossland, 2023).

599. Cappadocia in Turkey is famous for its "fairy chimney" rock formations, shaped by centuries of erosion and volcanic activity (Heller, 2015).

600. The Waitomo Glowworm Caves in New Zealand are illuminated by thousands of bioluminescent glowworms, creating a magical, starry-like display (Mat, 2023b).

601. The towering sandstone pillars in Zhangjiajie, China served as inspiration for the floating mountains in the movie "Avatar" (Quirk, 2018).

602. Eternal Flame Falls in New York is known for a natural gas leak behind a waterfall that causes a perpetual flame to burn. It does go out from time to time but is often relit by hikers (Woollaston, 2013).

603. Lake Hillier is a pink-colored lake on Middle Island in Western Australia (Klein, 2022). The algae species in the lake give the pink color.

604. The Avenue of the Baobabs is a grove of ancient, towering baobab trees lining a dirt road in western Madagascar (Grundhauser, 2014).

605. Cano Cristales in Colombia, often called the "River of Five Colors," is known for its vibrant aquatic plants that create a rainbow of colors in the water (Ettinger, 2023).

606. Kelimutu is a volcano in Flores, Indonesia, known for its three crater lakes, each with a different color (Algie, 2014).

607. The Valley of Flowers in Uttarakhand, India, is a UNESCO World Heritage Site known for its diverse alpine flora. It's also home to endangered animals such as the snow leopard and blue sheep (Negi, 2019).

608. The Wisteria Tunnels in Kawachi Fuji Gardens in Japan feature enchanting cascades of wisteria flowers forming two 328 ft (100 m) long colorful tunnels (Weiner, 2017).

609. Giant's Causeway in Northern Ireland is a natural wonder consisting of hexagonal basalt columns formed by volcanic activity (Mat, 2023a).

610. The Haiku Stairs in Hawaii, also known as the Stairway to Heaven, is a steep hiking trail with breathtaking views of Oahu. It consists of 3,922 steps (Groves, 2019).

611. The pink hue of the sand at Pink Sands Beach in the Bahamas is attributed to microscopic coral insects called Foraminifera (Stickles, 2019).

612. Shilin Stone Forest in China is a set of limestone formations resembling a forest of stone pillars (Mat, 2023c).

613. The Rakotzbrücke bridge in Kromlau, Germany creates a perfect circle when reflected in the water, earning it the nickname "Devil's Bridge" (Barnes, 2017).

614. Mosquito Bay in Vieques, Puerto Rico, is home to bioluminescent dinoflagellates, creating a surreal glow in the water at night (Galloway, 2014).

615. Aogashima is a volcanic island with a unique formation and a population living inside the crater (Lawson, 2022).

616. The Kawah Ijen Volcano in Indonesia is known for its mesmerizing blue flames caused by sulfuric gas igniting at night (Howard, 2014).

617. Tivoli Gardens in Copenhagen is one of the oldest amusement parks in the world, having been founded in 1843. It's said to have inspired not only Hans Christian Andersen but also Walt Disney (Clarke, 1993).

618. The Galápagos Islands are renowned for inspiring Charles Darwin's theory of evolution and are home to giant tortoises that can weigh up to 900 lbs (408 kg) (Gaeng, 2023b).

619. The Banaue Rice Terraces in the Philippines were carved by hand over 2,000 years ago by the Ifugao people. They are 4,900 ft (1,500 m) above sea level and it said that if its steps were placed end to end, it would encircle half the globe (*A guide to the Philippine rice terraces*, 2018).

620. Chichen Itza's El Castillo pyramid in Mexico is designed with astronomical precision. During the spring and fall equinoxes, a shadow forms a serpent descending the staircase (Konstie, 2023).

621. Baatara Gorge Waterfall in Lebanon descends into a sinkhole for 255m (837ft) and features three natural bridges (Sharif, 2017).

622. Blood Falls is a waterfall in Antarctica where iron-rich, saline water gives the appearance of flowing red blood (Ross, 2018).

623. The Museu do Amanhã in Brazil is an incredible museum that is known for its unusual design and is built from recycled materials (Matthews, 2016).

624. The most visited tourist destination is Paris with approximately 7.7 million tourists visiting the Louvre in 2022 alone (Gunarathne, 2023).

625. The Catacombs of Paris are underground ossuaries containing the remains of millions of people (Geiling, 2014).

626. Isla de las Muñecas or Island of Dolls in Mexico City is an uninhabited island that has dolls strung up all over by one man: Don Julian Santana Barrera (Thompson, 2022).

627. Bran Castle in Romania is often referred to as "Dracula's Castle," and is associated with the Dracula legend (R. Lewis, 2017).

628. Galesnjak islet in Croatia is nicknamed Love Island because it is shaped like a perfect heart (Reuters, 2023b).

Chapter20: Handy Human Body Facts

629. The human brain generates about 12–25 watts of electrical power when awake. That's enough to power a light bulb (Burket, 2019).

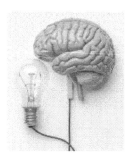

630. Your nose can remember 50,000 different scents (Tiwari, 2023).

631. The human heart can create enough pressure to squirt blood 30 ft (9 m)   (Magovern, 2012).

632. Humans shed about 600,000 particles of skin every hour (Marie, 2022).

633. The only part of the body without blood supply is the cornea. It gets oxygen directly through the air (Villazon, 2009).

634. The liver is the only organ that can regenerate itself (Sawyer, 2019).

635. Babies have more bones than adults! Babies have 300 bones while adults have 206 (Roland, 2019).

636. You use 200 muscles to take one step (Malcolm, 2015).

637. Your tastebuds are replaced every 2 weeks (Lockett, 2020).

638. The total surface area of the human lung is roughly the same size as a tennis court (Ananda Rao & Johncy, 2022).

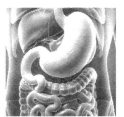

639. Human bones are ounce-for-ounce stronger than steel (Barna, 2018).

640. The average person will experience about 70,000 thoughts per day (Westenberg, 2017).

641. Your stomach lining replaces itself every few days to avoid being digested by the stomach's own enzymes (Gedney, 1983).

642. Human hair grows at a rate of about 0.2–0.7 in (0.5–1.7 cm) per month (Barrell, 2019).

643. The human body can produce 3.8 million new cells each second (Starr, 2021).

644. Your body contains enough iron to make a 3 in (7.6 cm) nail (Laun, n.d.).

645. The strongest and largest tendon in the human body is the Achilles tendon (O'Brien, 2005).

646. Assuming a maximum age of 75, the average person will spend about 25 years of their lives sleeping (Reville, 1996).

647. Every square inch of the human body has an average of 32 million bacteria on it (Fairfax, 2016).

648. They may not be heart-shaped, but your pupils do expand when you look at someone you love (Taylor, 2022).

649. Yawning is so contagious that even reading or thinking about yawning can trigger it (Gupta & Mittal, 2013).

650. Wisdom teeth are a vestigial feature in humans. In fact, because we don't need them anymore, some people are born without them (Roland, 2019).

651. There are more bacteria in your mouth than there are people in the world (Landers, 2019).

652. Laughter can boost your immune system, reduce stress, and even burn calories (Hajar, 2023).

653. Astronauts can grow up to two inches taller in space due to the absence of gravity compressing the spine (Kramer, 2013).

654. Fingernails grow faster than toenails, and the nails on your dominant hand typically grow faster (Adcox, 2018).

655. The average red blood cell lives for about 120 days, whereas taste buds have a lifespan of about 10 days before they're replaced.

656. Tears produced due to different emotions have distinct chemical compositions (Hussain, 2023).

657. Teenagers often experience increased appetite as the body requires more energy for growth and development (Lassi et al., 2017).

658. The air expelled during a sneeze can travel at a speed of up to 100 mph (161 kph) (University of Bristol, 2019).

659. The average speed of a fart leaving the human body is about 7 mph (11 kph) (Dove, 2015).

Chapter21: Surprising Ship Facts

660. The oldest known shipwreck dates back to around 2,400 years ago and was discovered in the Black Sea. The vessel is ancient Greek in origin (Rawlinson, 2018).

661. The first iron-hulled ship was built by Isambard Kingdom Brunel. The "Great Britain," was launched in 1843, revolutionizing ship construction (Warfield, 2017).

662. The Flying Dutchman is a legendary ghost ship doomed to sail the seas forever and is considered a harbinger of doom (Mambra, 2022a).

663. The largest container ship, the MSC Irina, can carry over 24,000 containers (Lindsay, 2023).

664. Nuclear-powered submarines can operate underwater for months without refueling (Shafran, 2023).

665. The Proteus and Triton were experimental submarines designed in 1960 to travel around the world submerged. This project was known as "Operation Sandblast" (Holzwarth, 2020).

666. Thor Heyerdahl and his crew crossed the Pacific Ocean on The Kon-Tiki, a balsa wood raft in 1947. He did this to prove that ancient civilizations could have made similar journeys (Fraga, 2022).

667. The sinking of the RMS Lusitania by a German U-boat in 1915 played a role in the United States entering World War I (McDermott, 2018).

668. The MV Wilhelm Gustloff, a German transport ship, holds the record for the largest loss of life resulting from the sinking of a single ship, with estimates ranging from 6,000 to 10,000 casualties (Uenuma, 2020).

669. Blackbeard, also known as Edward Teach, was one of the most infamous pirates, and his flagship was the Queen Anne's Revenge (Woodard, 2014).

670. Queen Anne's Revenge was a former French slave ship that he captured and outfitted with cannons (Woodard, 2014).

671. The USS Monitor and CSS Virginia fought in the first battle between ironclad warships during the American Civil War (Brimelow, 2021).

672. The USS Arizona, which was bombed during the attack on Pearl Harbor in 1941, burned for two and a half days before sinking (Mansoor, 2019).

673. Icebreakers, like the USCGC Polar Star, are designed to navigate through ice-covered waters and maintain access to polar regions (Hein, 2018).

674. Barnacles and other marine organisms attach themselves to ship hulls, a process called biofouling. Biofouling affects a ship's efficiency by producing more drag in the water (Adam, 2022).

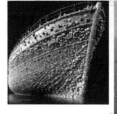

675. Trimaran warships have not one but three hulls, providing stability and speed (Singer, 2017).

676. Semaphore flags were historically used for long-distance communication between ships before the invention of the radio (Maguire, n.d.).

677. It's considered bad luck to rename a ship according to maritime superstitions (Ronca, 2015).

678. The Battle of Lepanto in 1571 was one of the largest naval battles in history, involving the Holy League and the Ottoman Empire (Brotton, 2020).

679. The Japanese battleship, Yamato, was the heaviest and most powerful battleship ever built. It weighed 70,000 tons fully loaded (Mizokami, 2021).

680. The SS United States, launched in 1952, still holds the Blue Riband for the fastest transatlantic ocean liner crossing from New York to Le Havre, France in less than 4 days (Ross, 2020).

681. "Zvezda" in Russia, has one of the world's biggest dry docks. It's fitted with four cranes and a unique hydraulic structure (Gain, 2020).

682. Admiral Lord Nelson, a British naval hero, died at the Battle of Trafalgar in 1805 and was famously preserved in a cask of brandy for his journey back to England (Stott, 2016).

683. The Mary Celeste, found adrift in 1872 with no crew on board, remains one of the greatest maritime mysteries (Blumberg, 2007).

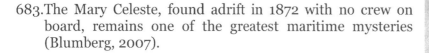

684. The Shackleton Expedition's ship, the Endurance, was trapped in Antarctic ice for 10 months in 1915, before

sinking (Wamsley, 2022).

685. The Essex, a whaling ship, inspired Herman Melville's novel "Moby-Dick" after it was attacked and sunk by a sperm whale in 1820 (King, 2013).

686. The SS Central America, carrying gold from the California Gold Rush, sank in a hurricane in 1857, resulting in a significant loss of treasure (Stone, 1992).

687. The Law of Salvage allows salvors to claim a reward for rescuing or recovering a ship or its cargo from peril (Menon, 2021).

688. Research is ongoing to develop ships powered by alternative energy sources like hydrogen fuel cells or electric propulsion for a zero-emission future (Madsen et al., 2020).

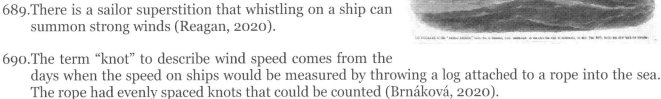

689. There is a sailor superstition that whistling on a ship can summon strong winds (Reagan, 2020).

690. The term "knot" to describe wind speed comes from the days when the speed on ships would be measured by throwing a log attached to a rope into the sea. The rope had evenly spaced knots that could be counted (Brnáková, 2020).

Chapter22: Fresh Farm Facts

691. Farming dates back around 12,000 years to the Neolithic or Agricultural Revolution when humans transitioned from hunter-gatherer lifestyles to settled farming communities (Blakemore, 2019).

692. Vertical farming involves growing crops in vertically stacked layers, often indoors, to maximize space and resource efficiency (Smit, 2023).

693. The most commonly consumed banana, called Cavendish, is sterile. It does not reproduce and is grown through cloning (Pearce, 2008).

694. Coffee is grown in a region called the "coffee belt," which spans the area between the Tropics of Cancer and Capricorn (Perez, 2023).

695. Sericulture involves raising silkworms on mulberry leaves to produce silk. This practice originated in ancient China and gave rise to the Silk Road (Cartwright, 2017).

696. Did you know that you don't need soil to grow plants? Hydroponic systems cultivate plants without soil, using nutrient-rich water solutions (Gulraiz, 2023).

697. Native American tribes practiced the "Three Sisters" agricultural method. It involved planting corn, beans, and squash together for mutual benefit (Hirst, 2012).

698. The decline of bee populations due to insecticide and pesticide use poses a threat to agriculture because bees play a crucial role in pollinating many crops (United Nations Environment Programme, 2019).

699. Seed banks, like the Svalbard Global Seed Vault, store seeds from diverse plant species to safeguard genetic diversity and ensure food security in the future (Gómez-Upegui & Liu, 2022).

700. Agroforestry is a practice that integrates trees and shrubs into agricultural systems (Agroforestry, 2019). By planting trees alongside crops, it is possible to protect the diversity of plants and animals and prevent soil erosion, thereby sustaining the ecosystem or farming operations.

701. Celebrated annually in the United States, National Agriculture Day honors the contributions of American agriculture (U.S. Department of Agriculture, 2023).

702. Bamboo is farmed for use in construction as it is flexible and strong (Weeden, 2020).

703. Aztecs in ancient Mexico used chinampas, artificial farming islands, to cultivate crops such as maize, beans, and squash in lake areas (Vasiloudis, 2021).

704. Ancient farmers used mud from the lake bottom to build chinampas and this enhanced soil fertility (Vasiloudis, 2021).

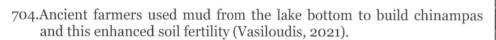

705. Some farmers follow moon planting calendars, believing that planting crops during specific lunar phases affects their growth (Gillette, 2022).

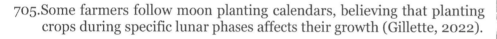

706. Experiments on the International Space Station involve growing crops in microgravity to study the challenges of space farming (Plackett, 2019).

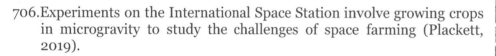

707. Qanats are ancient underground irrigation systems that bring water from aquifers to the surface (Jomehpour, 2009). Qanats collect water by tapping into underground aquifers. A mother well is dug at the source, from which a gently sloping tunnel is excavated horizontally into the hillside. This tunnel intercepts groundwater and channels it downhill, using gravity flow to bring the water to the surface for irrigation and drinking. By using this, even the driest regions like the middle of deserts in Iran can get water for farming.

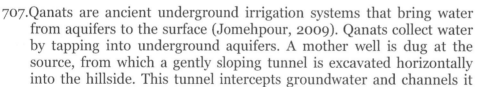

708. Broccoli is a human invention, created through centuries of selective breeding from wild cabbage (Orem, 2016).

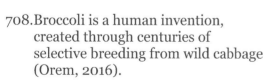

709. Kelp farming, or seaweed cultivation, is an emerging industry providing a sustainable source of food and biofuel (Sultana et al., 2022).

710. The first animals domesticated for food are thought to be sheep (Shindo, 2020).

711. Cotton was cultivated in ancient India, and it was known by the Romans as "the wool that grows on plants" (Sensei, 2021).

712. Jethro Tull, an English inventor, created the seed drill in the 1700s, revolutionizing planting efficiency (Bellis, 2015). A seed drill is a farming device that precisely plants seeds in the ground at a specific depth and spacing. It improves germination rates and crop yields by ensuring seeds are evenly distributed and covered with soil. This innovation, dating back to the 16th century, revolutionized agriculture by boosting efficiency and productivity.

713. Wasabi is particularly challenging to grow and traditionally cultivated in cool, flowing water (Petruzzello, 2020).

714. It takes 3 to 5 years for a cacao tree to mature and start producing cacao pods (Pearce Stevens, 2018).

715. Mushrooms don't contain chlorophyll and don't need sunlight for photosynthesis. This is why mushroom farming can be done indoors without light (Allman, 2012).

716. Over 90% of the world's 570 million farms are managed by families (Lowder et al., 2016).

717. Agriculture is one of the industries with the highest prevalence of child labor. An estimated 108 million children work in agriculture worldwide (United Nations, 2022).

718. Sugarcane is one of the fastest-growing plants in the world, capable of reaching heights of up to 10–24 ft (3–7 m) in just 6 to 18 months (Yamane, 2018).

719. To cater to the growing population, farmers need to increase their food production by 70% by 2025 (Daszkiewicz, 2022).

720. One acre of soybeans can produce 82,368 crayons (Piper, 2015)!

721. More than 1,000,000 acres of land have been planted with Christmas trees (Smith, 2023).

Chapter23: Powerful Poisons

722. Foxglove is poisonous when ingested in large amounts, but the digitalis glycoside it contains is used in heart medications (Cummings & Swoboda, 2019).

23. The Reef Stonefish is the world's most venomous fish, with 13 venomous spines on its dorsal fin (McGrouther, 2021).

24. Cone snails produce conotoxins that can be lethal to humans. However, some are being used in medical research for pain relief (Holmes, 2014).

725. Cone snails use a harpoon-like tooth to inject venom into their prey, paralyzing it before consumption (Holmes, 2014).

726. The blue-ringed octopus carries venom that can cause paralysis and death. There is no antivenom (Silver, 2020).

727. Monarch butterfly caterpillars feed on milkweed, making them toxic to predators (Vernimmen, 2019).

728. Assassin bugs inject toxic saliva into their prey, containing enzymes that break down tissues (Fischer et al., 2023).

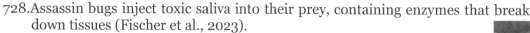

729. Giant Hogweed is a plant that has hollow stems containing poisonous sap. If it gets on your skin it can blister when exposed to sunlight (Charmley, 2022).

730. Harmful algal blooms, known as red tide, can produce toxins that contaminate shellfish, causing paralytic shellfish poisoning (PSP) (Hurley et al., 2014).

731. Naturally occurring in soil and rocks, arsenic can contaminate water sources and cause chronic poisoning (*Arsenic,* 2018).

732. Solanine, found in green potato sprouts, is toxic and can cause nausea, vomiting, and neurological symptoms (Smith, 2013).

733. Indigenous peoples of South America used curare, a plant-derived poison, for hunting by paralyzing prey (Blubaugh & Linegar, 1948).

734. Curare was found to inhibit breathing but not heart function. Thus, someone poisoned with curare can survive if their breathing can be supplemented (Blubaugh & Linegar, 1948).

735. Marine organisms can accumulate toxins from their environment, leading to bioaccumulation in the food chain as larger fish like tuna consume smaller fish (Debipersadh et al., 2023). For example, tuna are reported to have higher level of mercury accumulated in their bodies.

736. Approximately 25,000 people in the United States suffer venomous bites from insects and arthropods annually (Koehler & Diclaro II, 2022).

737. Jellyfish tentacles contain cnidocytes, specialized cells that release venom when triggered by touch (Frost, 2013).

738. Male platypuses have venomous spurs on their hind legs, capable of delivering a painful sting to predators or competitors (Hausheer, 2019).

739. Some caterpillars, like the saddleback caterpillar, have stinging hairs that release toxins causing skin irritation (Seldeslachts et al., 2020).

740. The bombardier beetle defends itself by ejecting a hot, toxic chemical spray that almost reaches boiling point from its abdomen (Chandler, 2015).

741. The crown-of-thorns starfish has venomous spines that can cause irritation and pain if touched (Hillberg et al., 2023).

742. Certain plants can accumulate toxic levels of manganese, affecting the health of livestock that graze on them (Kfle et al., 2020). An example of that is oleanders.

743. Arsenic compounds were historically used in medicine, including for the treatment of syphilis (Paul et al., 2022).

744. Mad honey is a result of bees feeding on the nectar of certain rhododendron flowers containing grayanotoxins. It causes symptoms like nausea and dizziness due to a drop in blood pressure (Chan et al., 2011).

745. Black widow spiders inject neurotoxic venom through their bites. While their bites can be painful, fatalities are rare (Williams et al., 2020).

746. The snake often considered to have the most toxic venom is the inland taipan, also known as the "fierce snake" (Munson, 2022).

747. The ancient Greeks tipped their arrows and spears with poisons and even poisoned water sources with toxic plants (Irvine, 2013).

748. Botulinum toxin, produced by *Clostridium botulinum* bacteria, causes botulism. It's also the main ingredient in Botox (*Botulism*, 2023). Botulism is a rare but serious illness caused by a toxin produced by bacteria. It can lead to muscle weakness, paralysis, and even death.

749. Lantana is a pretty flower to have in the garden but is toxic to humans and pets (Piro et al., 2018).

750. While we're talking about pretty flowers, Wisteria seed pods are also toxic to kids, dogs, cats, and horses (Morris, 2019).

751. In 1988, over 300,000 people in Shanghai became violently ill from eating blood clams. These clams tend to have high numbers of bacteria in them (Kantour, 2020).

752. Mistletoe is a plant with green leaves and white berries that grows on trees. It's often associated with holiday traditions and kissing rituals. But think twice about mistletoe in your decorations or at least keep them out of reach! The berries and leaves are quite toxic if ingested (Vallie, 2022a).

Chapter24: Stupendous Science Facts

753. Alexander Fleming discovered penicillin after returning to his work after a holiday. He noticed that mold inhibited bacterial growth in his Petri dishes (Tan & Tatsumura, 2015).

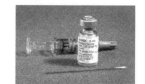

754. Edward Jenner developed the smallpox vaccine, the first successful vaccination, using material from cowpox lesions (Riedel, 2005).

755. Wilhelm Roentgen accidentally discovered X-rays while experimenting with cathode rays in 1895 (Schmidt, 2015). He noticed that a fluorescent screen in the room emitted light when he was making cathode rays in a cathode tube, which made him think there was an invisible ray that was coming from the cathode ray that penetrated the tubing and reached the screen.

756. Giovanni Aldini, conducted galvanic experiments on executed criminals, influencing the creation of Mary Shelley's "Frankenstein" (Ilott, 2022).

757. The Fibonacci sequence is a series of numbers in which each number is the sum of the two preceding ones (0, 1, 1, 2, 3, 5, 8, 13, ...) (Keatley, 2021).

758. The golden ratio, related to the Fibonacci sequence, is approximately 1.618. This ratio appears in shells, plants, and flowers (Keatley, 2021).

759. The Fermi Paradox questions why, given the vastness of the universe, we haven't observed extraterrestrial civilizations (Howell, 2018).

760. Schrödinger's Cat is a thought experiment that represents scientific theory. it basically proves that a cat is both dead and alive until you prove either to be true (Matthias, 2023).

761. The placebo effect demonstrates that patients can experience real improvements in health even when given a treatment with no active ingredients (Cherry, 2011).

762. Brain plasticity or neuroplasticity allows the brain to adapt and reorganize itself in response to learning, and experience (Puderbaugh & Emmady, 2023).

763. Phantom limb sensation occurs when amputees feel sensations or pain in limbs that are no longer present, revealing the brain's complex mapping of body parts (Dempsey-Jones, 2014).

764. The Mozart Effect suggests that listening to Mozart may temporarily boost spatial-

temporal reasoning skills (Jenkins, 2001).

765. The Tetris effect occurs when people spend a lot of time on a specific activity that it begins to pattern their thoughts, mental images, and dreams (Appleby, 2023).

766. Soap bubbles are like mini-rainbows. The colors you see are created when light reflects and bends through the bubble's surface (Allain, 2019).

767. You can write secret messages using lemon juice. When you heat the paper, the message appears (Murphy, 2011)!

768. The Slinky was accidentally created when an engineer knocked a spring off a shelf, and it "walked" down instead of falling (Fabry, 2015).

769. Post-it Notes were created by a scientist trying to make a strong glue. Instead, he ended up with a weak one, perfect for removable notes (Skonord, 2021).

770. Bananas contain a small amount of radioactivity due to the potassium isotope present in them (Schwarcz, 2018).

771. Helium balloons float because helium is lighter than air (Brain, 2000).

772. A lemon can act as a battery. If wires and electrodes(copper and zinc for example) are inserted into a lemon it can generate enough electricity to power a small LED light (Helmenstine, 2022).

73. Dmitri Mendeleev created the periodic table, arranging elements by atomic mass. Gaps in the table predicted the discovery of yet-to-be-known elements (Rouvray, 2019).

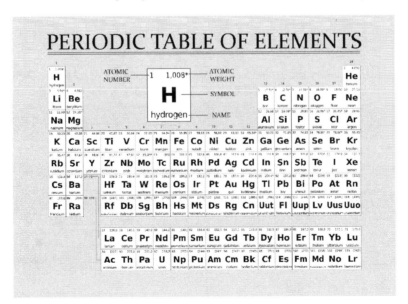

774. The first element identified in the history of chemistry was hydrogen in 1766 (Jolly, 2019).

775. The last naturally occurring element to be discovered was Francium in 1939 (Ballance, 2019).

776. The artificial element Oganesson (Og), with atomic number 118 was the last element to be added to the periodic table (Aron, 2016).

777. The rarest naturally-occurring element in the Earth's crust is astatine (Spalding, 2023).

778. The half-life of a radioactive element is the time it takes for half of a sample to decay (*Radiation studies - CDC: Properties of radioactive isotopes*, 2019).

779. The vibrant colors of a sunset are a result of the Earth's atmosphere scattering shorter wavelengths of light, leaving behind the warm hues (Castro, 2023).

780. It's impossible to burp in space. Due to the lack of gravity, the air does not rise as it would on Earth. Burping in space would lead to puking (Starr, 2018).

781. There is about 0.4 lbs or 200 g of salt (NaCl) in the average adult human body (Fisher, 2009).

782. Although oxygen gas is colorless, the liquid and solid forms of oxygen are blue (Helmenstine, 2019a).

783. A bucket of water contains more atoms than there are buckets of water in the Atlantic Ocean (Helmenstine, 2020).

Chapter25: Memorable Medicine and Disease Facts

784. Intractable singultus is a rare disorder that results in persistent and uncontrollable hiccups lasting more than 30 days (Cole & Plewa, 2020).

785. Alice in Wonderland syndrome is a neurological condition where individuals perceive objects or parts of their bodies as larger or smaller than they are (Stefan Bittmann et al., 2014).

786. Sir Isaac Newton, the genius who found gravity, once proposed the use of toad vomit to cure the plague (Fox, 2020).

787. The Hippocratic Oath dates back to 400 BCE in ancient Greece (Indla & Radhika, 2019). The Hippocratic Oath is a promise that doctors make when they enter the medical profession. They promise to help people feel better and stay healthy. They promise to be honest, keep secrets safe, and always try to do what's best for their patients.

788. Advances in medical technology have led to the development of artificial organs. However, their use is still being tested (Ackridge & Haney, 2019).

789. Ether and chloroform were among the first anesthetics used to induce unconsciousness during surgery (Abhyankar & Jessop, 2022).

790. The 1918 influenza pandemic, also known as the Spanish flu, remains one of the deadliest pandemics in history. Approximately 17.4 million people died (Roser, 2020).

791. Tuberculosis is a contagious bacterial infection that primarily affects the lungs, causing coughing and respiratory symptoms. Tuberculosis has been around for centuries. Approximately 25% of the

current population carries the bacterium that causes Tuberculosis (*Tuberculosis*, 2018).

792. The Zika virus, transmitted by mosquitoes, gained global attention for its association with birth defects (Rawal et al., 2016).

793. The world's oldest known prescription is a Sumerian tablet from around 2100 BCE (Norn et al., 2005).

794. The first successful human organ transplant was a kidney transplant performed in 1954 by Dr. Joseph Murray and Dr. David Hume (Nordham & Ninokawa, 2021). Kidneys filter blood, remove waste, regulate fluid balance, and produce urine to eliminate toxins from the body.

795. James Lind, a British naval surgeon, discovered the link between vitamin C deficiency and scurvy (White, 2016). Scurvy, historically, has been associated with significant death tolls, particularly among sailors during long sea voyages due to the lack of fresh fruits and vegetables.

796. Louise Brown, born in 1978, was the world's first baby conceived thro ugh in vitro fertilization (IVF) (Nugent, 2018).

797. Inoculation, an early form of vaccination, was practiced in ancient China and India to prevent smallpox (Boylston, 2012). Smallpox is a contagious viral disease causing fever, rash, and sometimes death. Inoculation is introducing a weakened form of a disease to stimulate immunity, protecting against future infections.

798. Karl Landsteiner discovered human blood groups in 1901, leading to safer blood transfusions (Schwarz & Dorner, 2003).

799. Warfarin, a widely used blood thinner a medicine that helps stop blood from clotting too much and keeping people safe from dangerous blood clots, was initially developed as a rat poison in the 1940s (Lim, 2017).

800. African trypanosomiasis, or sleeping sickness, is a parasitic disease transmitted by tsetse flies, causing fever, headaches, and neurological symptoms (Dunn et al., 2019).

801. Kuru is a rare neurodegenerative disorder, characterized by tremors, loss of coordination, and cognitive decline, transmitted through cannibalistic rituals in Papua New Guinea. (Liberski, 2013).

802. Rye grains are hardy cereal grains used for baking bread, distilling whiskey, feeding animals, and as a cover crop. Ergotism, historically known as St. Anthony's Fire, results from consuming rye grain contaminated with fungus. It can cause hallucinations and gangrene (Horgan, 2020).

803. Trimethylaminuria, or "Fish Odor Syndrome," is a metabolic disorder causing individuals to emit a strong fishy odor in their breath, sweat, and urine (Arseculeratne et al., 2007).

804. The Jumping Frenchmen of Maine is a rare neurological condition characterized by exaggerated startle reflexes and involuntary, impulsive movements (Saint-Hilaire et al., 1986).

805. Fatal Familial Insomnia is a rare hereditary prion disease that leads to progressive insomnia, hallucinations, coma, and eventually, death (Khan & Bollu, 2019).

806. In the 19th century, cocaine-infused tooth drops were commonly used to soothe teething infants (Ní Chríodáin, 2018).

807. It wasn't unusual for people to consume tapeworm-infested pills to achieve weight loss, not realizing the potential health risks (Winterman, 2013).

808. In medieval Europe, ointments containing human fat were believed to have healing properties (Gillan, 2022).

809. In the 1800s, dentistry was quite crude. If you wanted a perfect set of teeth, you would probably have to wear dentures made from someone else's teeth (Vučković, 2019).

810. The "Sushruta Samhita," an ancient Indian text, describes various surgical procedures, including plastic surgery techniques, dating back over 2,000 years (Loukas et al., 2010). The image shows Sushruta Samhita texts written in the 7 palm leaves.

811. During the Napoleonic Wars, military surgeons used maggots to clean wounds, Maggots used in Napoleonic wars to clean wounds, consuming dead tissue, and prevent infection. They are still sometimes used today (Tarshis, 1938).

812. Moss, known for its absorbent properties, was used as a primitive form of bandage in ancient cultures (Boissoneault, 2017).

813. In ancient Greece, snail syrup was recommended as a remedy for coughs and respiratory ailments (James, 2015).

814. Cotard Delusion, also known as Walking Corpse Syndrome, is a rare psychiatric disorder where individuals believe they are dead or do not exist (Grover et al., 2014).

815. Vampires or allergic to the sun? Solar Urticaria is a rare condition where individuals develop hives, itching, and redness when exposed to sunlight (Harris et al., 2020).

Chapter26: Timeless Treasure Facts

816. sarcophagus was not just one but three gold caskets inlaid with precious stones. It's the innermost casket that we are most familiar with as it's solid gold (Cummins, 2015).

817. The Florentine Diamond is a 127.37-carat, nine-sided diamond, worth $20 million and is believed to have belonged to the Medicis. It has been missing since 1919 (East, 2021)(The image is a close replica)

818. The Crown Jewels of Iran, housed in the Central Bank of Iran, include the Darya-ye Noor, one of the largest pink diamonds in the world (Cathaway, 2019). The size is 41.40 mm × 29.50 mm × 12.15 mm (1.630 in × 1.161 in × 0.478 in) and weighs around 182 metric carats.

819. The Cullinan Diamond was the largest gem-quality diamond ever discovered at 3,106 carats (Roos, 2022). Roughly, an average engagement ring has about 1 carat, so one can make 3,106 rings from the Cullinan Diamond.

820. The Great Star of Africa, cut from the Cullinan Diamond, is the largest clear-cut diamond in the world, weighing 530.2 carats. It's part of the British Crown Jewels (Roos, 2022).

821. The Peacock Throne, commissioned by Shah Jahan in 1628, was the greatest accumulation of precious gemstones in the 17th Century (Tola, 2019).

822. The Golden Buddha in Thailand is the largest Buddha made of solid gold, weighing an incredible 5.5 tons (Williams, 2018).

823. The Golden Buddha was accidentally discovered in 1955 when the plaster covering cracked revealing the gold inside (Williams, 2018).

824. The rumored "Nazi Gold Train" from World War II, filled with treasures, is said to be hidden in a collapsed tunnel in Poland (Halpern, 2016).

825. The Staffordshire Hoard, found in England in 2009, is the largest collection of Anglo-Saxon gold and silver metalwork ever discovered (Kennedy, 2009).

826. The Staffordshire Hoard contained 1500 individual pieces and added up to about 11 lbs (5 kg) of gold. It's valued at £3.3 million ($4.18 million) (Kennedy, 2009).

827. The Rosetta Stone, housed in the British Museum, played a crucial role in deciphering Egyptian hieroglyphs (Solly, 2022).

828. The Irish Crown Jewels, stolen in 1907, have never been found and the case remains unsolved (Fox, 2022).

829. The Dresden Green Diamond, a rare 41-carat green diamond, is considered one of the most valuable diamonds in the world (Volandes, 2022).

830. The Oak Island Money Pit in Nova Scotia has been the focus of treasure hunters for almost three centuries. There has been evidence of something buried on the island, but no treasure has been found (Taylor-Lehman, 2021).

831. The curse of Oak Island says that seven men must die before the treasure is found.

So far, there have been six deaths associated with the treasure (Taylor-Lehman, 2021).

832. The Lost Dutchman's Gold Mine in Arizona is a legendary treasure said to be hidden in the Superstition Mountains. No one has found it yet (Gleason, 2018).

833. Cocos Island, an island off Costa Rica is said to be the place where the Treasure of Lima is hidden. Despite the rumors, it has not been found (Dobson, 2019).

834. The Great Train Robbery in the UK in 1963 saw 15 armed men steal millions of pounds from a postal train. Only 10% of the money was recovered (Hagen, 2014).

835. The SS Central America sank in 1857 with a fortune in gold. In 1988, the shipwreck was discovered, and a part of its treasure was recovered (McLeod, 2014).

836. Gangster Dutch Schultz supposedly buried a treasure in upstate New York. He spoke about the hoard on his deathbed in 1935 but never revealed the exact location (Herbert, 2021).

837. The Yamashita Treasure, rumored to be hidden by the Japanese during World War II, remains a subject of speculation and treasure hunting in the Philippines (Cosep, 2020).

838. In 2014, a couple discovered a cache of gold coins worth $10 million buried on their property in California (Vives, 2014).

839. Captain Kidd, a notorious pirate, is said to have buried treasure along the coasts of the Americas, but none of his caches have been definitively found (Blakemore, 2015).

840. In 2019, an artist known as "Satoshi's Treasure" initiated a global treasure hunt for Bitcoin, with a prize pool worth millions (Moos, 2019).

841. The Golden Apple Tale is referred to as an "armchair treasure hunt" that was released in 1982 by author Cam Kaskgn. The golden apple has not been found (Konecny, 2017).

842. El Dorado, the legendary city of gold in South America, has never been conclusively located (Jago Cooper, 2013).

843. There is speculation that El Dorado may have referred to a person and not a place at all (Jago Cooper, 2013).

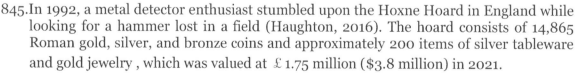

844. The San Jose Galleon, a Spanish ship carrying 200 tons of gold, silver, and emeralds, was discovered off the coast of Colombia in 2015 (Cormack, 2023).

845. In 1992, a metal detector enthusiast stumbled upon the Hoxne Hoard in England while looking for a hammer lost in a field (Haughton, 2016). The hoard consists of 14,865 Roman gold, silver, and bronze coins and approximately 200 items of silver tableware and gold jewelry , which was valued at £ 1.75 million ($3.8 million) in 2021.

846. Homeowners renovating an old house in France in 2019 discovered a collection of 239 gold coins hidden within the walls (McGreevy, 2021).

Chapter27: Historically Peculiar Facts

847. Napoleon Bonaparte, often thought of as short, was actually about 5 feet 6 inches (1.68 meters) tall, which was average for his time (Zelazko, 2023).

848. In 1932, Australia declared war on emus after the birds damaged crops. The "war" involved soldiers armed with machine guns trying to control the emu population (Mirzai, 2023a).

849. Albert Einstein's brain was stolen by the pathologist who performed his autopsy in 1955. It was later discovered and returned for scientific study (Kremer, 2015).

850. Oliver Cromwell, The Lord Protector of England, Ireland, and Scotland in the 17th century had his head posthumously severed and spiked, before being stolen (Stolze, 2014).

851. In 1647, the English Parliament, led by Oliver Cromwell, banned Christmas celebrations (Stoyle, 2021).

852. Abraham Lincoln may have been the President of the United States but he started out as a licensed bartender (Cavanaugh, 2013).(The image of bartender is not Abraham Lincoln)

853. Speaking of strange floods, in 1814, a huge vat of beer burst in London, causing a flood that killed eight people (Eschner, 2017).

854. During the Renaissance, ground-up mummies were used in paint for their rich brown color. It was aptly called "Mummy Brown" (Eveleth, 2014).

855. An artificial eye, believed to be the oldest found, was discovered in a woman's grave in Iran. It dates back to 2900–2800 BC and was made of bitumen and animal fat.

856. The Anglo-Zanzibar War in 1896 holds the record as the world's shortest war, lasting only 38 minutes (Hudson, 2019).

857. On the other hand, the Dutch-Scilly War lasted 335 years but had no battles or deaths (Young-Brown, 2016).

858. A dog tax was passed in England in 1796, possibly as a way to discourage ownership or generate revenue for the state (Tague, 2008).

859. The Blue Cross Medal was awarded to a Great Dane named Juliana during World War II. She peed on an incendiary bomb, extinguishing it and saving many lives (Martin, 2021).

860. In 1386, a pig was executed in France. It was found guilty of fatally wounding a child (Vatomsky, 2017).

861. The day it was announced that World War II ended, Russia ran out of vodka as everyone drank it in celebration (Bell, 2016)!

862. Tablecloths were originally designed to be used as one big napkin for everyone to use (Campbell, 2019).

863. Tyrian purple was the color of royalty and it was illegal for anyone else to use the color (Gorvett, 2023).

864. The ancient Maya played a ball game called "Pitz," which is similar to soccer but players could not touch the ball with their hands or feet (Davies, 2012).

865. In ancient Maya culture, crossed eyes were considered beautiful. Parents would sometimes make their babies stare at objects hung above their noses to encourage their development (Veliz, 2021).

866. In ancient Athens, citizens could vote to ostracize a politician by writing their name on a shard of pottery. The person with the most votes would be banished for 10 years (Gannon, 2020).

867. In Victorian times, people used fans to convey subtle messages (Starp, 2018).

868. Aeschylus, the ancient Greek playwright, died when an eagle dropped a tortoise on his bald head, mistaking it for a rock to crack open the shell (Karasavvas, 2018).

869. Bulgarian dissident Georgi Markov was assassinated in 1978 using a specially crafted umbrella that injected a small pellet of ricin into his leg (Kesteven & Stott, 2021).

870. Louis XIX of France had one of the shortest reigns in history, lasting only 20 minutes during his unconventional coronation in 1830 (Weeks, 2013).

871. The Voynich Manuscript, an illustrated codex from the 15th century, contains an undeciphered code that has baffled cryptographers and historians for centuries (Gaspard, 2023).

872. The Battle of the Oranges is an annual event in Ivrea, Italy, where participants reenact a medieval battle using oranges instead of weapons (Mooallem & Frazzetta, 2023).

873. Postmortem photography was popular in the Victorian era. Families would dress up and pose for pictures with deceased loved ones (B. Bell, 2016).

874. In 1979, "Disco Demolition Night" at a baseball game in Chicago turned into a riot as fans destroyed disco records on the field (Lynskey, 2023).

875. In the 1930s, some London apartments featured "baby cages"–small, suspended outdoor containers–to allow infants to get fresh air and sunlight (Lee, 2021).

876. The fear of being buried alive during the Victorian era led to the invention of safety coffins with bells and escape mechanisms (Tarazano, 2018).

877. In the Victorian era, men with mustaches used special cups. The mugs had a guard on them, preventing mustaches from dipping into their tea (Frost, 2017).

Chapter28: Superb Survival Facts

Surprising Survivors

878. During the Marathon des Sables in 1994, Mauro Prosperi got lost in the Sahara Desert and survived by drinking his own urine and eating bats (Cocozza, 2023).

879. However, drinking urine is dehydrating and you should never eat wild bats as they carry diseases that can be passed to humans (Wilson, 2008).

880. In 2003, Aron Ralston survived being trapped in a canyon by amputating his own arm after it became pinned by a boulder (Barkham, 2010).

881. Alexander Selkirk, a Scottish sailor, survived 4 years alone on an uninhabited island in the Pacific Ocean in the early 18th century, inspiring the novel "Robinson Crusoe" (Selcraig, 2005).

882. In 1971, Juliane Koepcke survived a plane crash in the Amazon rainforest, falling almost 10,000 ft (3 km) and trekking through the jungle for 11 days before rescue (Armitage, 2022).

883. In 1972, Dougal Robertson and his family survived for 38 days on a life raft in the Pacific Ocean after their yacht was sunk by killer whales (Williams, 2009).

884. Violet Jessop survived the collision of the Olympic in 1911, the sinking of the Titanic in 1912, and the Britannic in 1916, earning her the nickname "Miss Unsinkable" (Charleston, 2022).

885. Richard Proenneke spent over 30 years living alone in the Alaskan wilderness, documenting his experience in the film "Alone in the Wilderness" (Kuroski, 2021).

886. In 2012, Jose Alvarenga survived 438 days adrift in the Pacific Ocean, sustaining himself on fish, birds, and turtles (Franklin, 2015).

887. In 2013, Harrison Okene survived for 72 hours in an air pocket of a sunken ship off the coast of Nigeria before being rescued (Brock, 2013).

888. Oxana Malaya survived 5 years living with dogs in Ukraine, exhibiting feral behavior until her discovery in 1991 (Grice, 2006).

889. In 2006, Ricky Megee survived 71 days in the Australian Outback by living off wild plants and insects after his car broke down (Jones, 2006).

890. An Indian soldier, Hanamanthappa Koppad, survived being buried in an avalanche for 6 days, using a tent to create an air pocket (Banchiri, 2016).

Facts to Help You Survive

891. Use reflective materials, mirrors, or bright-colored clothing to signal for help in open areas (James, 2020).

892. Have a plan for rationing food to ensure it lasts until rescue (Scouter, 2020).

893. Learn how to create improvised tools from available resources, such as sharpening a stick for a makeshift knife (Black, 2016).

894. Identify alternative water sources, such as dew on leaves, rainwater, or collecting water from plants (Cunningham, 2023a).

895. If in a snowy environment, understand how to build an emergency snow shelter like a snow cave or quinzee (Powell, 2019).

896. Protect your eyes from snow blindness by creating improvised snow goggles (Hutchison, 2020).

897. Create makeshift snowshoes from materials like branches or clothing to make travel in deep snow more manageable (MacWelch, 2021).

898. A solar still is a device that can use the sun to purify water for drinking from unlikely sources like seawater and the ground (Cunningham, 2023b).

899. You can construct a solar still with minimal materials to collect water through condensation (Cunningham, 2023b).

900. Manage sea sickness by keeping your eyes on the horizon, staying hydrated, and avoiding heavy or greasy meals (Marcin, 2018).

901. If in cold water, adopt the Heat Escape Lessening Position (HELP) to reduce heat loss and increase your chances of survival (Singh, 2019).

902. Without food, your body will start to utilize stored energy. Conserve energy by avoiding unnecessary physical activity (Vandette, 2020).

903. Practice controlled breathing techniques to reduce stress and conserve energy (Jenkins, 2016).

904. The human body can survive longer without food than without water (Vandette, 2020).

905. If you find a water source, follow it downstream. This can lead to civilization and provide a consistent source of water (Xavier, 2013).

906. If in a hot and dry environment, do not travel during peak heat hours. Travel when it's cooler or even at night if possible (Myers, 2016).

907. Unless you are an expert, it's safer to avoid mushrooms altogether to prevent poisoning (Ranadheera, 2023).

908. Insects are generally safe to eat as long as they are not hairy, but don't eat beetles or worms (Bennett, 2016).

Chapter29: Odd Oil, Gas, Rock, Mineral and Jewel Facts

909. The formation of fossil fuels, such as oil and natural gas, began millions of years ago from the remains of plants and marine organisms (Nunez, 2019).

910. Sapphires, often associated with a blue hue, come in various colors such as pink, yellow, and green. There are even multicolored ones called parti sapphires (Agarwal, 2021).

911. Oil reservoirs are typically found underground in porous rocks, such as sandstone or limestone, where oil accumulates in the pore spaces (Speight, 2012).

912. Hydraulic fracturing, or fracking, is a method of extracting natural gas or oil from underground shale formations. It involves injecting a mixture of water, sand, and chemicals into the rock to create fractures, allowing the trapped gas or oil to flow to the surface for collection.

913. Russia is a major producer of diamonds, producing 41.92 million carats of diamonds in 2022 (Statista Research Department, 2023).

914. Quartz comes in many varieties, including amethyst (purple), citrine (yellow), and rose quartz (pink) (Rybnikova, 2021).

915. Geodes are hollow rock formations that contain crystals inside. They form when minerals slowly crystallize within a cavity in a rock usually caused by lava (Baggaley, 2012).

916. In some oil-producing regions, natural gas is burned off (flared) into the atmosphere as a byproduct of oil extraction (Thurber, 2019).

917. Some minerals exhibit fluorescence, emitting visible light when exposed to ultraviolet light. Examples include fluorite and calcite (King, 2016).

918. "Blood diamonds" or "conflict diamonds" are diamonds mined in war zones and sold to finance armed conflicts (Baker, 2019).

919. Pearls are formed inside oysters as a defense mechanism against irritants(Eisenstadt, 2021).

920. Methane hydrates, also known as "fire ice," are ice-like structures containing methane molecules and are found in permafrost and deep-sea sediments (Weissert, 2021).

921. Methane hydrates are only stable under specific conditions of low temperature and high pressure, making them challenging to study and extract (Weissert, 2021).

922. There are over 4,000 known minerals, each with its unique composition and properties (*Minerals and gems,* 2017).

923. Jade comes in two varieties: jadeite and nephrite. Both are prized for their toughness and unique colors (Benbrook, 2022).

924. Crude oil goes through a refining process to separate different components, including gasoline, diesel, jet fuel, and various petrochemicals (Hayes, 2020b).

925. In ancient times, oil seeps were used for medicinal purposes. People believed that oil from certain seeps had healing properties (Progga, 2020).

926. Some sapphires exhibit a phenomenon called asterism, creating a star-like pattern on the surface when cut into a cabochon shape (Sedawie, 2019b).

927. Some gems, like rutilated quartz, contain needle-like inclusions of titanium dioxide(Arem, 2022).

928. Some meteorites contain gem-quality crystals, such as olivine, and are cut and polished to create unique extraterrestrial gemstones (Sedawie, 2019a).

929. Although we have peridot here on Earth, some peridot crystals are found in meteorites originating in space (Sedawie, 2019a).

930. Petroleum jelly is used for moisturizing skin, protecting minor cuts, soothing chapped lips, preventing diaper rash, and aiding wound healing. Petroleum jelly, a byproduct of oil refining, was discovered when workers noticed a waxy substance accumulating on oil rigs (Polizzi, 2023).

931. Some gems contain trace amounts of radioactive elements, making them luminescence (Groat, 2017).

932. Large copper deposits found in porphyry rocks are formed by the intrusion of magma and subsequent mineralization. They are considered evidence of failed eruptions (Chiaradia & Caricchi, 2022).Copper is used for many purposes such as electric wire.

933. Lithophonic rocks ring like a bell when you strike them (Varga, 2022). There are ringing rocks in Pottstown, Pennsylvania.

934. Halite is made up entirely of sodium chloride and is therefore called rock salt (King, n.d.).

935. Certain minerals, like fluorite, can change color when exposed to different types of light, making them like natural mood rings (Koester, 2020).

936. Crude oil is classified as either "sweet" or "sour" based on its sulfur content. Sweet crude has low sulfur, while sour crude has higher sulfur levels (Fernando, 2003). Sulfur content of oil is important because high sulfur oil(sour oil) is acidic and tend to damage pipelines faster.

937. Crude oil can range in color from black to yellow, depending on its composition (Liberto, 2023).

938. Lapidary, refers to working with gemstones. Lapidarists cut and shape crude gems (Clark, 2023).

939. Karlu Karlu or the Devil's Marbles are large, rounded granite boulders located in Australia's Northern Territory. The rocks were formed by erosion but look as if they were placed in specific spots (Patowary, 2014).

Chapter30: Incredible Insect Facts

940. Insects have been around for a very long time. Fossil evidence suggests that they appeared around 420 million years ago during the Devonian period (Guarino, 2022). They appeared roughly 200 million years earlier than dionsaurs!

941. In ancient Egypt, the fly represented perseverance, and golden fly amulets were awarded to officials in the army (Woodcock, 2021).

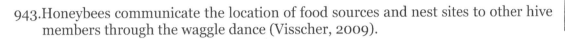

942. Most insects undergo metamorphosis, a process involving distinct stages such as egg, larva, pupa, and adult (Hadley, 2019).

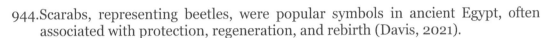

943. Honeybees communicate the location of food sources and nest sites to other hive members through the waggle dance (Visscher, 2009).

944. Scarabs, representing beetles, were popular symbols in ancient Egypt, often associated with protection, regeneration, and rebirth (Davis, 2021).

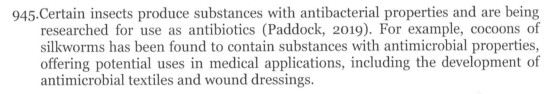

945. Certain insects produce substances with antibacterial properties and are being researched for use as antibiotics (Paddock, 2019). For example, cocoons of silkworms has been found to contain substances with antimicrobial properties, offering potential uses in medical applications, including the development of antimicrobial textiles and wound dressings.

946. Entomophagy, the consumption of insects, is common in many cultures worldwide (Olivadese & Dindo, 2023). Crickets and grasshoppers are among the most commonly consumed insects. They can be roasted, fried, or ground into a powder to be used in baking or as a protein supplement.

947. Scientists have identified 1611 edible insect species thus far (Van Itterbeeck & Pelozuelo, 2022).

948. Cockroaches are known for their resilience and adaptability. They can survive extreme conditions, including radiation exposure up to 15 times longer than humans (Stanton, 2019).

949. Fleas possess incredible jumping abilities, with some species able to jump up to 220 times their body length (Castillo, 2013).

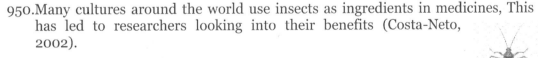

950. Many cultures around the world use insects as ingredients in medicines, This has led to researchers looking into their benefits (Costa-Neto, 2002).

951. Some ants have a buddy system with aphids. The ants protect the aphids from predators, for example ladybugs, and get to feed on the honeydew produced by the aphids (Hadley, 2009).

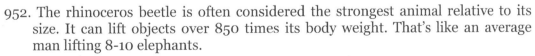

952. The rhinoceros beetle is often considered the strongest animal relative to its size. It can lift objects over 850 times its body weight. That's like an average man lifting 8-10 elephants.

953. Bees have been observed to exhibit individual personalities. Some are more adventurous and others are more cautious in their behaviors (Solon, 2019).

954. Spider silk is incredibly strong for its weight. It is one of the strongest materials found

in nature, with some varieties being stronger than steel of the same diameter.

955. Some species of assassin bugs even wear the desiccated exoskeletons of their victims for camouflage (Stromberg, 2012a).

956. Butterflies engage in puddling, a behavior where they gather on damp soil to extract salts and minerals (Shea, 2014).

957. Insects perceive colors differently than humans. Bees, for example, see in the ultraviolet spectrum, allowing them to detect patterns on flowers that are invisible to humans (Glass, 2005).

958. Bark beetles pick trees based on the presence of fungus. If the tree has a fungal infection, it will be easier for them to feed on (Wetzel, 2023).

959. Darkling beetles in the Namib Desert use their bodies to collect water from fog (Nørgaard & Dacke, 2010).

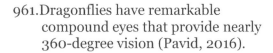

960. Tiger moths have evolved the ability to detect bat echolocation calls and respond with sonar jamming, disrupting the bats' ability to locate and capture them (Corcoran et al., 2011).

961. Dragonflies have remarkable compound eyes that provide nearly 360-degree vision (Pavid, 2016).

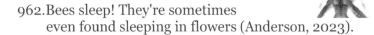

962. Bees sleep! They're sometimes even found sleeping in flowers (Anderson, 2023).

963. The praying mantis is capable of rotating its head 180 degrees to scan its surroundings and locate prey (Jain, 2021).

964. Insects don't have blood. They have something called hemolymph and it's usually clear, yellow, or green depending on what the insect feeds on (Brown, 2013).

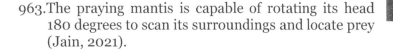

965. Jewel beetles possess specialized infrared receptors, allowing them to detect the heat emitted by forest fires. They need these because their larvae need to develop in trees killed by fire (Schneider et al., 2015).

966. Cicadas undergo long periods of underground development before emerging in synchronized mass emergences, called "broods." These occur in 13- or 17-year cycles (Alger, 2013).

967. Many insects such as treehoppers and crickets communicate through vibrations produced by various body parts (Joyce & McQuay, 2015).

968. The Lord Howe Island stick insect, commonly known as "land lobsters" is considered one of the rarest insects in the world (Black, 2013).

969. Stink bugs only release a bad smell when threatened and don't stink all the time (Shipman, 2019).

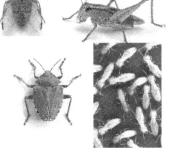

970. A termite queen can lay 30,000 eggs per day (Kapelari, 2020)!

Chapter31: Perfect Pirate Facts

971. The word "pirate" is derived from the Latin word "pirata," which means sea-robber (Burke, 2017). The Golden Age of Piracy occurred during the late 17th and early 18th centuries, when piracy flourished in the Caribbean and Atlantic.

972. Privateers were essentially privately-owned ships authorized by a government during times of war to attack and capture enemy vessels. Buccaneers, on the other hand, were essentially pirates who operated outside the law, who operated in the Caribbean Sea during the 17th century (Lane, 2019). When they received "letter of marque" from the government, pirates were authorized to attack ships of hostile countries.

973. Blackbeard, one of the most infamous pirates, was actually named Edward Teach (Ullian, 2019).

974. Pirates often operated in loose alliances or fleets, working together to raid merchant ships and coastal towns.

975. Many pirate crews operated under a set of rules known as the Pirate Code. This code governed behavior, division of plunder, and more (Gatto, 2023).

976. The pirate Black Bart Roberts captured over 400 ships during his career, making him one of the most successful pirates in history.

977. Pirates traded their stolen goods at taverns either to pay for their tabs, or to exchange them for money (Goodall, 2022).

978. Certain ports, like Nassau in the Bahamas, became infamous as pirate havens during the Golden Age of Piracy (Cartwright, 2021).

979. Pirates had various methods of execution for those who broke the Pirate Code, including marooning and keelhauling (Adamson, 2004).

980. Keelhauling involved tying a person up with weights and tossing them off the ship while still tied to the ship. They would be dragged under the hull until death (Adamson, 2004).

981. Some pirates believed that getting a tattoo of a pig and a rooster on their feet would prevent them from drowning (Kruse, 2016).

982. Pirates had their own songs, often sung to boost morale and pass the time during long sea voyages (Vallar, n.d.-a).

983. Many pirates considered Fridays to be an unlucky day to set sail (Truewalker, 2018).

984. Blackbeard supposedly used to drink a mixture of rum and gunpowder (Pierini, 2022). Pirates often drank rum, which was readily available from Caribbean sugar plantations, leading to the association between pirates and rum

985. Henry Morgan, initially a privateer, turned to piracy in the authorized by England to attack Spanish ships and territories in Caribbean. He won many battles against Spanish, and the fiercest battle was the attack on Panama where he led 30 English and French ships with large amounts of pirates. He later became the Lieutenant Governor of Jamaica (Johnson, 2019) because of his contribution to England.

986. Pirates were known for their unique style. They dressed to show off their wealth and this included clothes, weapons, hairstyles, and jewelry (Vallar, n.d.-b).

987. The youngest pirate ever known was named John King. He was approximately 10 or 11 years old when he joined Sam Bellamy's crew (McDermott, 2022).

988. It was not unusual for pirates to have hooks for hands and wooden legs as they would lose them in battle (Christensen, 2023).

989. Pirate crews slept in hammocks because only the captain had sleeping quarters (Dalton, 2018).

990. Most pirates had families and were not bachelor seafarers as most people think (Hanna, 2017).

991. Pirates would maroon troublesome crew members on a deserted island (Adamson, 2004).

992. Pirates drank grog which was a mixture of rum and water but sometimes included lime and sugar (Frank, 2022).

993. Pirate treasure was not just gold and silver. They stole food, books, fabric, and spices which all held value (P. Smith, 2013).

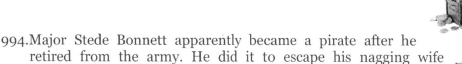

994. Major Stede Bonnett apparently became a pirate after he retired from the army. He did it to escape his nagging wife (Crawford, 2007).

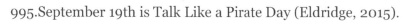

995. September 19th is Talk Like a Pirate Day (Eldridge, 2015).

996. Merchant sailors usually joined pirate crews after they were captured. They got better pay (Jacque, 2007).

997. Pirates used secret hideouts, known as pirate havens or pirate dens, to repair their ships, divide plunder, and lay low from authorities. The havens include the island of Madagascar: The island was a favored destination for pirates seeking refuge from European authorities, with pirate communities established along its coastlines.

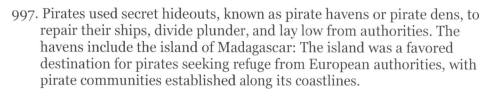

998. "Black Sam" Bellamy was known as both the wealthiest pirate in recorded history and the "Robin Hood of the Sea" (Bridges, 2021). One estimation suggests that he had about $163 million of wealth.

999. The Whydah Gally is the world's only authenticated pirate ship (Davis-Marks, 2021). Whydah Gally was a trade ship fitted with 18 guns, used for trading goods like gold, slaves, ivory, indigo, etc. from Africa to Caribbean. On her second sail, she was chased for 3 days and captured by Black Sam Bellamy. Sam used her as his flagship until it sank with him at the coast of Massachusetts.

1000. When the Whydah sank, it was the most significant pirate loot ever seized, containing an estimated 4.5 to 5 tons of treasure. This hoard included vast amounts of indigo, ivory, gold, and between 20,000 to 30,000 British pounds sterling, which was organized into 180 bags, each weighing 50 pounds (approximately 23 kg)

1001. There are still pirates sailing the seas right now (Villalba, 2021)!

Chapter32: Nifty National Park Facts

1002. Yellowstone National Park stretches across three states: Wyoming, Montana, and Idaho (Lesso, 2022).

1003. Yellowstone is also home to the largest supervolcano on the continent (Ravilious, 2016).

1004. At 692 mi (1,114 km) the Yellowstone River is the longest undammed river in the contiguous United States (Sather, 2022).

1005. The Galápagos National Park in Ecuador features the Galápagos Islands. The islands are located at the confluence of three ocean currents (Huseynli, 2023).

1006. Jiuzhaigou Valley National Park in China is known for its colorful lakes, including the famous five-coloured lake (Bongso-Seldrup, 2019).

1007. The Torres del Paine National Park in Chile features iconic granite towers that attract climbers and hikers from around the world (Duggan, 2018). The tallest part, the Paine Grande peak, is about 2,884 m (9,462 feet).

1008. Fiordland National Park is home to Lake Hauroko, the deepest lake in New Zealand (Christopher, 2023).

1009. The Fiordland National Park also has the Milford Track, known as the "finest walk in the world" (Roy, 2018).

1010. Kakadu National Park in Australia is home to the largest collection of Aboriginal rock art, some of which dates back over 20,000 years (Van Dongen, 2007).

1011. The Picos de Europa National Park in Spain contains one of the deepest limestone gorges in Europe, the Cares Gorge (Brett, 2023).

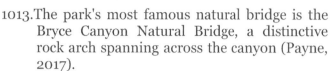

1012. Bryce Canyon National Park in Utah has the largest collection of hoodoos on the planet (Payne, 2017).

1013. The park's most famous natural bridge is the Bryce Canyon Natural Bridge, a distinctive rock arch spanning across the canyon (Payne, 2017).

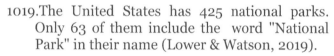

1014. Bryce Canyon has been designated as an International Dark Sky Park, making it an excellent destination for stargazing (Carter, 2023).

1015. The Kruger National Park in South Africa is home to the majority of the world's black and white rhino population (Hossain, 2023).

1016. Rocky Mountain National Park in the USA has over 300 mi (480 km) of hiking trails, including the famous Longs Peak trail (Kwak-Hefferan, 2023).

1017. Trail Ridge Road, which traverses the park, is the highest continuous paved road in North America. It reaches an elevation of 12,183 ft (3,713 m) (Kwak-Hefferan, 2023).

1018. There are over 6,000 National Parks across the globe (Ezzo, 2023).

1019. The United States has 425 national parks. Only 63 of them include the word "National Park" in their name (Lower & Watson, 2019).

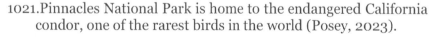

1020. Hawaii Volcanoes National Park is home to two of the world's most active volcanoes, Kilauea and Mauna Loa (*Everything to know about Hawaii Volcanoes National Park,* 2019).

1021. Pinnacles National Park is home to the endangered California condor, one of the rarest birds in the world (Posey, 2023).

1022. The park's most famous talus cave is Bear Gulch Cave, where visitors can explore the subterranean environment filled with rock formations and passageways (Posey, 2023).

1023. Tongariro National Park in New Zealand features Mount Ngauruhoe, which served as the inspiration for Mount Doom in the "Lord of the Rings" trilogy (Hill, 2020).

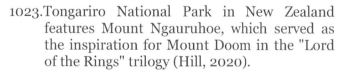

1024. Dolomiti Bellunesi National Park in Italy is home to the Dolomite mountains, known for their pink hue during sunrise and sunset, a phenomenon known as the "Enrosadira" (Lorenzi, 2021).

1025. Kaziranga National Park in India hosts two-thirds of the world's great one-horned rhinoceroses (Singh, 2016).

1026. Located in the Amazon rainforest, Madidi National Park is one of the most biodiverse places on Earth and is home to numerous rare and unique species (Shearman, 2022).

1027. Fuji-Hakone-Izu National Park is the most visited national park in Japan, having approximately 70 million visitors in 2021 (Arba, 2023).

1028. The Russian Arctic National Park was established in 2009 to protect the natural and cultural heritage of the region (Howard, 2016).

1029. Saguaro National Park in Arizona is named after the iconic Saguaro cactus (Waterman, 2021).

1030. In Death Valley National Park, Racetrack Playa is a dry lakebed known for its mysterious moving rocks (Byrd, 2021).

1031. Several cases of Hantavirus Pulmonary Syndrome were linked to Yosemite National Park in 2012. It was caused by rodent-infested lodgings (Núñez et al., 2014).

1032. Torres del Paine National Park in Chile is home to the Milodon Cave, where remnants of a Mylodon sloth were found (Anda, 2018).

Chapter33: Wicked Weapons and Weaponry

1033. Leonardo da Vinci designed various weapons, including a tank-like vehicle (Mitchell, 2022). The tank-like vehicle was designed to wield 32 cannons!

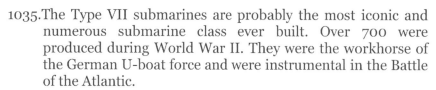

1034. First used in World War I, flamethrowers were employed to clear enemy trenches (Fratus, 2022).

1035. The Type VII submarines are probably the most iconic and numerous submarine class ever built. Over 700 were produced during World War II. They were the workhorse of the German U-boat force and were instrumental in the Battle of the Atlantic.

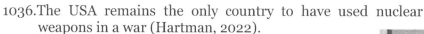

1036. The USA remains the only country to have used nuclear weapons in a war (Hartman, 2022).

1037. Invented by Richard Gatling, the Gatling Gun was an early form of a rapid-fire weapon (Martin, 2016).

1038. Napoleon Bonaparte's strategic use of artillery played a key role in his military successes (Dean, 2019). Briefly, he mobilized the artilleries and concentrated artillery fires to the enemy defense lines, supporting infantry advances.

1039. The English longbow had a longer range and higher accuracy than many contemporary weapons like crossbows. It played a crucial role in medieval battles, notably during the Hundred Years' War (Hickman, 2007). The English longbow offered a higher rate of fire and longer range, crucial for open-field tactics, but required years of training and significant physical strength. The French crossbow, more powerful and easier to learn, excelled in penetrating armor but was slower to reload and more expensive to produce and maintain.

1040. The Roman Gladius was a short, double-edged sword used by Roman soldiers (Esposito, 2017).

1041. The ancient Greeks developed the phalanx formation, a military tactic where soldiers formed a closely packed, shield-bearing line (Chan, 2011).

1042. Advanced guidance systems have made smart bombs capable ofprecision strikes, a common feature in modern warfare (Mahnken, 2011).

1043. Cyberweapons play a critical role in modern conflicts, with the ability to disrupt communication networks and sabotage critical infrastructure (Hempel, 2023).

1044. The Active Denial System is a non-lethal weapon that uses directed energy to create a sensation of intense heat, compelling individuals to move away (Verger, 2020). One described the concentrated beam sent by the weapon felt as an oven put in front of his face.

1045. The Chemical Weapons Convention, signed in 1993, prohibits the development, production, and use of chemical weapons (Khan, 2022). The chemical weapons banned include mustard gas, which was used in WWI and already banned in 1925.

1046. International efforts have been made to prevent the weaponization of space (Yan, 2022).

1047. Throughout history, civilizations such as the Carthaginians and ancient Indians used war elephants as formidable beasts of war (Burstein, 2020).

1048. Some people still use slingshots for hunting small game (Ganger, 2021). The speed of the shot can reach 216kph(135mph) in some comparable to some small firearms.

1049. The Aboriginal Australians had specialized fighting boomerangs with blades 18 in (46 cm) long (Watson, 2016).

1050. The Viking battle axe had handles up to 7 ft (2 m) long (Neilsen, 2016).

1051. Some indigenous tribes use blowpipes to shoot poison-tipped darts for hunting and warfare (Jett, 1970). The speed of darts fired from blowpipes can get as fast as about 108-324kph(68-203mph).

1052. Ninja stars, or shurikens, were used by ninjas in ancient Japan for both throwing and hand-to-hand combat (Ashcraft, 2015).

1053. Nunchucks were originally agricultural tools.

1054. Barbed wire became a military obstacle in World War I, used to create entanglements in trenches (Moore, 2018).

1055. The chakram, a flat, circular throwing weapon, was used by Indian warriors with unique throwing techniques (Singh Madra, 2008).

1056. Wind and fire wheels were ancient Chinese weapons with circular sharp blades similar to the chakram.

1057. The Apache revolver was a unique weapon, combining a knife with a single-shot revolver and brass knuckles (McCollum, 2015).

1058. The first version of a torpedo was used in the 16th century and was nothing more than barrels of gunpowder on a long stick (Beatty, 2023).(The image is a 19th century torpedo made with the same concept.)

1059. Bolas consist of weighted balls connected by cords, historically used by indigenous peoples in South America for hunting (Dow, 2012).

1060. Alfred Nobel, the inventor of dynamite, believed that his invention would bring about world peace by making war too destructive (Tägil, 1998).

1061. Improvised incendiary weapons, Molotov cocktails are made from a glass bottle filled with flammable liquid (Helmenstine, 2019b).

1062. The khopesh is an ancient Egyptian sword characterized by its sickle-shaped blade, used for slashing and hooking (Cambal, 2022).

1063. Massive railway guns, mounted on steam trains, were developed for long-range bombardment during the late 19th and early 20th centuries (Simpson, 2015).

Chapter34: Progressive Population Facts

1064. The global population is rapidly aging, with the number of people aged 65 and older expected to double by 2050 (Yuzbasioglu, 2021).

1065. The world's median age is around 30 years (Ritchie & Roser, 2019).

1066. Japan has one of the oldest populations, with a median age of over 48 years (Ausubel, 2020).

1067. Niger in West Africa has one of the youngest populations, with a median age of around 15 years (Ausubel, 2020).

1068. Demographic projections indicate that the world's population could reach around 9.7 billion by 2050 (United Nations, 2019).

1069. China is experiencing rapid population aging due to its one-child policy and increasing life expectancy (Walsh, 2023).

1070. The one-child policy in China was adopted in 1979 to address concerns of population growth (Kane & Choi, 1999).

1071. Bulgaria has one of the fastest population declines in the world, driven by emigration and low birth rates (Alexander, 2017).

1072. The population of the United Arab Emirates is made up of 89% immigrants (*Immigration by country 2022*, 2023).

1073. There is a strong correlation between education levels, especially for women, and fertility rates. Higher education often corresponds to lower fertility (Weinberger, 1987).

Chapter35: Daring Dangerous Animals

1074. The sting of Africanized honey bees is not worse than other bees but more of them will attack a threat (P. Wood, 2022).

1075. Stonefish can blend into their surroundings, resembling rocks on the ocean floor (Khalil et al., 2018). And their spines are poisonous and deadly.

1076. Hippos are responsible for approximately 500 human deaths a year while lions are only responsible for 22 (Williams, 2023).

1077. Piranhas are not as dangerous as you think. They will only go after large prey if it's already dying or dead (Thompson, 2014).

1078. Piranhas are also known to exhibit cannibalistic behavior, especially when food is scarce (Thompson, 2014).

1079. Killer whales have complex social structures and are known to teach hunting techniques to their young (Stiffler, 2011).

1080. Leopards are known to carry prey into trees for safekeeping (Okafor, 2022).

1081. African rock pythons are impressive swimmers and can stay submerged to hide themselves from threats (Sherman, n.d.).

1082. Asian giant hornets, also known as "murder hornets," are capable of decimating entire honey bee colonies within hours (Learish, 2020).

1083. Wolverines are known to eat the bones and teeth of their prey (Bradford, 2014).

1084. Crocodiles and alligators use a "death roll" to dismember large prey by spinning underwater (Fish et al., 2007).

1085. The rhyme "Red touches black, you're okay Jack; Red touches yellow, you're a dead fellow" is often used to distinguish venomous coral snakes from harmless look-alikes (Kingsley, 2022b).

1086. While generally peaceful, giant pandas have strong jaws and sharp claws, making them potentially dangerous when threatened (Mulroy, 2022a). Giant panda's biting force is roughly 6 to 10 times stronger than humans.

1087. Baboons have powerful jaws and sharp teeth, and in certain situations, they can become aggressive (Kingsley, 2022a).

1088. The Portuguese Man-of-War is not a single organism but a colony of specialized polyps (*Portuguese man-of-war | National Geographic*, 2010). Despite its appearance resembling a single organism, it is actually a colonial organism made up of numerous individual animals called zooids, working together as a single unit. It has tentacles that sting just like jellyfish do.

1089. Some giant centipedes have venom that can cause pain, swelling, and, in rare cases, allergic reactions in humans (Jarai, 2020).

1090. Stingrays have a venomous barb on their tails, and injuries can occur if stepped on or disturbed (Gotter, 2018).

1091. Spitting cobras can accurately spray venom into the eyes of predators or threats (Greenbaum, 2017).

1092. Bullet ants are named for the intense pain of their sting, which has been compared to being shot (McClure, 2023).

1093. In 2011, a Burmese python in the Everglades was found to have ingested a 76 lbs (35 kg) deer whole (Alsup & Gast, 2011).

1094. The Portia jumping spider mimics the vibrations of prey on other spiders' webs to lure them toward them before pouncing (Aldhous, 1996).

1095. Vampire bats are the only mammals to survive solely on blood (Sartore, 2011).

1096. Some starfish can extend their stomachs outside their mouths to digest prey externally (Hall, 2022).

1097. *Loa loa* is a parasitic nematode that is spread by deer flies. They migrate through the human eye, causing vision problems and discomfort (Pallara et al., 2022).

1098. *Ophiocordyceps unilateralis*, a parasitic fungus, infects ants and takes control of their nervous system, leading them to a specific location for the fungus to grow (Lu, 2019).

1099. Owls regurgitate pellets containing indigestible parts of their prey, such as bones and fur (Lewis, 2015).

1100.Certain flies lay eggs on living animals, and the hatched maggots burrow into the flesh to feed (Francesconi & Lupi, 2012).

1101.Some shark species practice intrauterine cannibalism, where larger embryos consume their smaller siblings within the mother's womb (Chapman et al., 2013).

1102.Vultures, when threatened, may vomit as a defense mechanism, releasing a foul-smelling substance to deter predators (Langley, 2013).

1103.Scorpions cause approximately 2,600 deaths a year globally (Feola et al., 2020).

1104.A shark was once found with a full suit of armor in its stomach (Sorren, 2014)!

Chapter36: Sensational Senses

1105.The sense of smell is closely linked to memory and emotion. Certain scents can evoke powerful memories and trigger emotional responses, often more effectively than other senses (Thomas & Papesh, 2022).

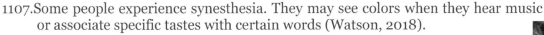

1106.The brain can integrate information from multiple senses simultaneously, allowing for a comprehensive perception of the environment (King, 2017).

1107.Some people experience synesthesia. They may see colors when they hear music or associate specific tastes with certain words (Watson, 2018).

1108.Pit vipers can detect infrared radiation, allowing them to "see" the heat emitted by warm-blooded prey even in complete darkness (Fang, 2010).

1109.The platypus has electroreceptors in its bill, allowing it to detect the electric fields generated by the muscle contractions of its prey (Gregory et al., 1987).

1110.Binocular vision is what enables humans to perceive depth and judge distances accurately (Bedinghaus, 2019).

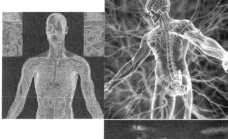

1111.Elephants can communicate over long distances by producing and sensing seismic waves through the ground (Mortimer et al., 2021). The sound cannot be heard by humans. Some suggest they can communicate with each other over a several kilometers of distance.

1112.Electronic skin, or e-skin, is a flexible and stretchable material embedded with sensors that can detect pressure, temperature, and other tactile stimuli (Bunea et al., 2021).

1113.Electronic noses mimic the sense of smell and are used in various industries for quality control, environmental monitoring, and detecting specific odors (Wilson, 2013).

1114.Genetic differences play a significant role in determining our taste perception (Bartoshuk, 2000).

Chapter37: Wonderfully Weird Sea Creature Facts

1115. A "globster" is a term used since 1962 to describe unidentified organic masses that wash ashore (Djossa, 2018).

1116. *Dendrogramma enigmatica* is a mysterious, deep-sea creature that resembles a mushroom and was discovered off the coast of Australia (Nuwer, 2014).

1117. Parrotfish have fused teeth that resemble a beak, which they use to scrape algae from coral reefs, contributing to coral sand production (Adey & Loveland, 2007).

1118. Hatchetfish have thin bodies and flattened sides that reflect light, allowing them to remain nearly invisible when viewed from the side (Rosenthal et al., 2017).

1119. The hatchetfish also has bioluminescent organs on its belly making it nearly invisible when viewed from below (Crew, 2014).

1120. Decorator crabs camouflage themselves by attaching various objects, such as sponges and algae, to their exoskeletons (Langley, 2018).

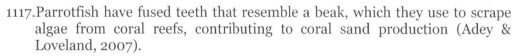

1121. Some sea cucumbers can expel their string-like internal organs as a defense mechanism. They can regenerate (Okada & Kondo, 2019).

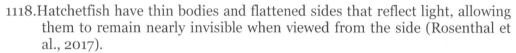

1122. The red-lipped batfish has bright red lips and walks on the ocean floor using its pectoral fins (Green, 2023).

1123. The dorsal fin of Remora fish has become specialized to form a suction plate to allow attachment to other marine animals (Heimbuch, 2013).

1124. Giant tube worms thrive near hydrothermal vents on the ocean floor which are known to reach 750°F (400°C) (Stover, n.d.).

1125. Also known as the blue dragon, *Glaucus atlanticus* is a small sea slug that feeds on venomous jellyfish and saves their stinging cells for use later (Heimbuch, 2022).

1126. Octopuses have 3 hearts. Two hearts pump blood to the gills, while the third pumps it to the rest of the body. When an octopus swims, the heart that delivers blood to the body stops, making swimming extremely exhausting for them.

1127. Yeti crabs have long, hairy pincers and are named after the mythical Yeti due to their furry appearance (Brauner, 2020).

1128. The humpback anglerfish uses bioluminescent bacteria in a lure attached to its forehead to attract prey in the dark depths of the ocean.

1129. The cookie-cutter shark takes circular bites out of larger animals and boats using its specialized teeth (Márquez, 2023b).

1130. The vampire squid, despite its name, doesn't suck blood but does live 2000–3000 ft (610–914 m) underwater (Perez, 2017).

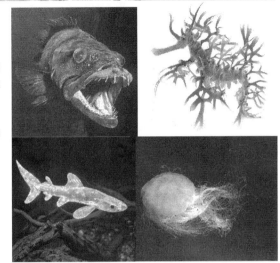

1131. The leafy sea dragon resembles floating seaweed and is a master of camouflage (Loy, 2022).

1132. The Antarctic toothfish has antifreeze proteins in its blood that prevent its body fluids from freezing in subzero temperatures.

1133. The lion's mane jellyfish has tentacles that can reach lengths of 120 ft (37 m) (Gaeng, 2022b).

1134. The luminous lanternshark has bioluminescent organs along its body, allowing it to glow in the dark (Stegman, 2022).

1135. The hairy frogfish can open its mouth and swallow prey in just 1/6000th of a second, making it one of the fastest eaters in the animal kingdom.

1136. The leaf sheep sea slug has a unique appearance with branch-like structures on its back, resembling a tiny, colorful sheep (Caballar, 2021).

1137. Opisthoproctus soleatus, known as the barreleye fish, boasts transparent fluid-filled domes for eyes, allowing it to see both above and forward in the deep ocean depths.

1138. The ocean sunfish is the heaviest bony fish and has a distinctive flattened body, resembling a large floating head (*Ocean sunfish (Mola) | National Geographic*, 2010). The largest ocean sunfish can reach weights of up to 2,300 kg (5,070 lbs).

1139. The bacteria found near hydrothermal vents thrive at extreme temperatures and form symbiotic relationships with other marine animals (Hall, 2019). By the way, hydrothermal vents can reach up to around 350℃ because of the high water pressure and heat by the underlying magma.

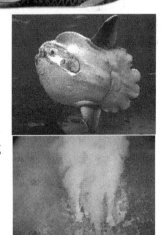

1140. The sea pig is a deep-sea sea cucumber with tube-like legs and a plump, pig-like appearance, which it uses to move along the ocean floor.

1141. In 2012, a giant baseball-sized eyeball washed ashore on a beach in Florida. The eyeball, initially a mystery, belonged to a large swordfish (Gardner, 2012).

1142. The painted hornshark is a new species with strange human-like molar teeth (Price, 2023).

1143. The frilled shark has 300 teeth arranged in 25 rows, making it one of the most toothy creatures in the ocean.

1144. The Green Bomber Worm has green, bioluminescent "bombs" that it releases to deter predators (Yong, 2009a).

Chapter38: Booming Brain Facts

1145. "Brain freeze" occurs when something cold touches the roof of the mouth, causing blood vessels to constrict and then rapidly dilate (Gora & Nierenberg, 2023).

1146. Despite representing only about 2% of body weight, the brain consumes around 20% of the body's total energy (Heid, 2018).

1147. The average adult human brain weighs about 3 lbs (1.4 kg) (Cherry, 2019).

1148. Human brains have tripled in size over the course of human evolution (Macdonald, 2018).

1149. Short-term memory has a limited capacity and can typically hold around seven items at a time (Mcleod, 2022).

1150. Mirror neurons fire both when an individual performs an action and when they observe someone else performing the same action (Acharya & Shukla, 2012).

1151. The brain can reorganize itself after injuries, and other areas may compensate for damaged regions (Castellanos et al., 2011).

1152. In the 19th century, Phineas Gage survived a severe brain injury when a metal rod pierced his frontal lobe. His personality changed dramatically, revealing the frontal lobe's role in personality and behavior (Cherry, 2022).

1153. Microglia, the brain's immune cells eliminate weak or unused connections, contributing to neural efficiency (Fliesler, 2012).

1154. The brain itself does not feel pain because it lacks pain receptors (Basbaum, 2014).

Chapter39: Majestic Meteors

1155.Before entering the Earth's atmosphere, it's called a meteoroid. As it travels through the atmosphere and produces light, it's called a meteor. If it survives the journey and reaches the Earth's surface, it's termed a meteorite (*Meteors and meteorites - NASA Science*, 2017).

1156.It's estimated that 6,100 meteorites fall to Earth every year (Choi, 2022).

1157.The Perseids is an annual meteor shower that occurs between mid-July and late August caused by the debris of the Swift-Tuttle comet (*Perseids - NASA Science*, n.d.).

1158. The Leonids meteor shower is associated with the debris from the Tempel-Tuttle comet and occurs annually between November and December (Rao, 2023).

1159.Meteor storms are rare but intense events where a significant number of meteors are observed within a short period, often exceeding 1,000 meteors per hour (Rao, 2022).

1160.In 2013, a meteor exploded in the atmosphere over Chelyabinsk, Russia, producing a bright flash and damaging over 7,000 buildings (Rawlings, 2013).

1161.The meteor exploded with the energy of around 500 kilotonnes of TNT (Sample, 2013).

1162.Meteoroids travel through space at extremely high speeds, often exceeding 25,000 mph (40,000 kph) (Marshall, 2019).

1163.Meteorites have been discovered on other planets and moons within our solar system, including Mars and the Moon (Jenniskens, 2013).

1164.Meteors leave behind a trail of ionized gas and tiny particles called meteoric smoke, which can affect radio communications (Cohen et al., 1989).

1165.Some cultures, like the Aborigines of Australia, believe that meteorites have special properties, and pieces of meteorites are used as talismans (Bevan & Bindon, 1996).

1166.Ancient Egyptians used meteoric iron for tools and weapons, recognizing its unique properties (Schultz, 2013).

1167.Scientists have found evidence of water molecules in some meteorites (Sawyer, 1999).

1168.Meteors begin to burn up and produce light at altitudes of around 50–75 mi (80–120 km) above the Earth's surface (Klesman, 2020).

1169. The Moon lacks a significant atmosphere, so meteors strike its surface far more often, giving it the cratered appearance that it has (Jones, 2023).

1170. Theoretically, meteorite impacts in oceans can generate tsunamis, causing significant coastal destruction (Wünnemann & Weiss, 2015).

1171. Meteorites often exhibit magnetic properties, and scientists study these to understand the conditions of the early solar system (Bryson et al., 2015).

1172. Meteorites have been examined for signs of extraterrestrial life, such as microbial fossils (van Loon, 2005).

1173. Impact glass, or tektites, is created by the intense heat of a meteorite impact (Rochette et al., 2021).

1174. In March 2003, a meteor shower hit the densely populated neighborhood of Park Forest in Chicago (Koppes, 2004).

1175. Meteorites have a distinct smell, described as similar to sulfur or gunpowder (Frąckiewicz, 2023a).

1176. The theory of panspermia suggests that life on Earth could have originated from organic materials brought by meteorites (Spall, 2023).

1177. Ann Hodges is the only person who has ever been hit by a meteorite (Eschner, 2016).

1178. If you ever find a meteorite that has just fallen, don't touch it with your bare hands! The microbes from your hand will contaminate the meteorite (Fries, 2023).

1179. In 2012, a meteorite was used to create a limited-edition wine called Meteorito in Chile (Thornhill, 2012).

1180. Meteorites are sometimes incorporated into jewelry, creating unique and extraterrestrial pieces (Frąckiewicz, 2023b).

1181. In the Nördlingen region of Germany houses and buildings were constructed using stones from the local Ries Crater formed by a meteorite impact (Vickery, 2017).

1182. The stones used in the buildings of Nördlingen have tiny diamonds in them, making the town a famous tourist destination (Vickery, 2017).

1183. The first recorded meteorite fall in history is believed to be the Ensisheim meteorite, which fell in Alsace, France, in 1492 (Sauers, 2023).

1184. Naveen Jain has a $5 million meteorite collection and says he has almost one of every meteorite type ever found (Greenwald, 2012).

1185. Iron meteorites, composed mostly of iron-nickel alloys, exhibit a distinctive Widmanstätten pattern when cut, revealing their crystalline structure (Lotzof, 2018).

Chapter40: Totally Truthful Toilet Facts

1186.The largest toilet roll ever made is equivalent to 95,000 rolls of regular toilet paper (Price-Williams, 2020).It was 2.97 m (9 ft 8.9 in) in diameter, and 2.59 m (8.6feet) high.

1187.The longest toilet queue consisted of over 756 people in Brussels (Reuters, 2009).

1188.On average, a person uses about 57 sheets of toilet paper per day (*Toilet paper fun facts*, 2019).

1189.It takes approximately 384 trees to make one person's lifetime supply of toilet paper (*Toilet paper fun facts*, 2019).

1190.Researchers were able to collect feces samples from an ancient latrine in Cyprus that was used by the Crusaders more than 800 years ago (Nuwer, 2013).

1191.NASA has developed new toilets for the International Space Station. Urine is filtered and reused while solid waste is stored in a canister that burns during re-entry to Earth (*Boldly go! NASA's new space toilet offers more comfort, improved efficiency for deep space missions,* 2020).

1192.Medieval castles had "garderobes," which were essentially small rooms with openings, allowing waste to drop into moats or cesspits (Blankenship, 2023).

1193.Sir John Harington, a godson of Queen Elizabeth I, is credited with inventing the flush toilet in 1596. He called it the "Ajax" (Castelow, 2015).

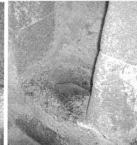

1194.The first flushing toilet in the White House was installed during the presidency of Millard Fillmore in 1853 (Brockell, 2021). 1195.The first patent for perforated toilet paper was filed by Seth Wheeler in 1891 (Willett-Wei, 2015).

1196.The orientation of toilet paper (over or under) has sparked debates for years. The patent from 1891 shows it in the "over" position (Willett-Wei, 2015). 1197.Japan is known for its high-tech toilets, and the first electric toilet seat with a built-in bidet was introduced in 1967 (Scheer, 2021).

1198.In the age of smart homes, there are toilets that respond to voice commands, allowing users to control various functions hands-free (Doe, 2021).

1199.World Toilet Day is observed on November 19th (United Nations, n.d.).

1200. The World Toilet Foundation was founded in 2001 to improve global sanitation and toilet conditions globally (*World Toilet Organization*, n.d.).

1201. There are novelty toilet-themed cafés in Canada and America where diners sit on toilets and eat from toilet-shaped bowls (Godden, 2017).

1202. An art installation called "America" featured a fully functional toilet made of 18-karat gold (Associated Press, 2023).

1203. The modern portable toilet, commonly seen at outdoor events, was invented by George Harding in the 1960s (*Who invented the porta potty? | Wonderopolis*, n.d.).

1204. In Japan, some public restrooms have devices that play flushing sounds to mask toilet noises for users' privacy (Fluhr, 2016).

1205. Solar-powered toilets are designed to operate in areas without access to traditional sanitation infrastructure, providing sustainable solutions (Kone, 2021).

1206. Some innovative toilets convert human waste into biogas or electricity, contributing to renewable energy sources (Kone, 2021).

1207. Waterless composting toilets are used in remote areas of Australia to conserve water and minimize environmental impact (Dowse, 2019).

1208. Squat toilets, where users squat rather than sit, are common in many Asian countries and are believed to have health benefits (Chen et al., 2021).

1209. There is a Toilet Island in Belize (Mafi, 2017).

1210. It's a misconception that toilet water flows clockwise in the Southern Hemisphere and counterclockwise in the Northern Hemisphere (Castro, 2011).

1211. An ancient flush toilet has been discovered in China which is almost 2,400 years old (Subramaniam, 2023).

1212. The remains of a 165-year-old toilet from the Great Exhibition of 1851 have been uncovered in London's Hyde Park (Mansfield, 2016).

1213. Innovative toilets with integrated sinks allow users to wash their hands with water that then fills the tank for the next flush (Rani, 2022).

1214. During the Renaissance, toilet chairs with a hole in the seat became popular. Some were designed to fit over chamber pots (Sharrett, 2014). 1215. In some regions worldwide, there are places where flushing toilet paper is discouraged, and instead, it's disposed of in a bin provided in the bathroom (Romano, 2017).

1216. Romans used communal sponges on sticks, called "tersorium," as a form of ancient toilet paper (Silver, 2020).

Chapter41: Petrifying Parasites and Microbes

1217.*Naegleria fowleri*, known as the brain-eating amoeba, is found in freshwater lakes around the world. It enters through the nasal passages and causes a rare but deadly brain infection (Pervin & Sundareshan, 2020).

1218.The pork tapeworm (*Taenia solium*) can cause neurocysticercosis if larvae infect the brain, leading to seizures (García et al., 2003). So never eat pork raw or not cooked with enough heat.

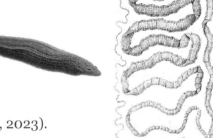

1219.Some parasitic flatworms can regenerate into complete organisms from fragments (Torgan, 2015). Planarians are an example of that.

1220.Microbes, including bacteria and fungi, have been found to survive, adapt, and thrive in space environments (Koehle et al., 2023).

1221.Guinea worm larvae infect humans through contaminated water, growing into long worms that emerge painfully from skin blisters (*Guinea worm disease - General information - Frequently asked questions (FAQs)*, 2020). 1222.Some bacteria can assist in the desalination process by removing salt from water, potentially addressing water scarcity issues (Amezaga et al., 2014).

1223.Parasitic wasps inject their eggs into caterpillars, and the wasp larvae consume the caterpillar from the inside as they grow (Simon, 2014b). The images show a parasitic wasp and its white tiny cocoons growing out from a worm.

1224.Modified viruses, used as vectors, are employed in gene therapy to deliver therapeutic genes into cells (Lundstrom, 2018). It is designed so that the virus injects healthy proper DNAs to substitute abnormal DNAs that are causing diseases.

1225.Certain bacteria can break down oil spills through a process called bioremediation (Perdigão et al., 2021).

1226.*Cryptosporidium* is a protozoan parasite that can cause waterborne illnesses. It's resistant to chlorine, making water treatment challenging (Chauret et al., 2001). Water treatment plants use alternative methods like UV radiation or filtration to remove or inactivate the parasite.

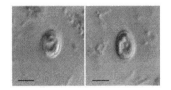

1227.Bacteria can form biofilms, which are communities of microorganisms encased in a slimy matrix, and they are often resistant to antibiotics (Shree et al., 2023).

1228.Viruses that infect bacteria are called bacteriophages (Kasman & Porter, 2020). Researches are ongoing to kill bacteria using viruses.

1229.Viruses exhibit various shapes, enabling them to be classified into three main groups: helical, polyhedral, spherical, or

complex (Gelderblom, 1996).

1230. Microbes known as extremophiles can survive and thrive in extreme conditions, such as high radiation, acidity, or salinity (Irwin, 2020). An example of that kind is tardigrade.

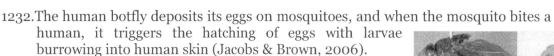

1231. *Vibrio fischeri*, a bioluminescent bacterium, forms symbiotic relationships with the Hawaiian bobtail squid, providing camouflage with their light (Tischler et al., 2019).

1232. The human botfly deposits its eggs on mosquitoes, and when the mosquito bites a human, it triggers the hatching of eggs with larvae burrowing into human skin (Jacobs & Brown, 2006).

1233. Certain bacteria can generate electricity through the production of microbial fuel cells (Lal, 2013).

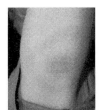

1234. The number of microbial cells in and on the human body is estimated to outnumber human cells by 8 trillion (Sender et al., 2016).

1235. The bacteria in your gut are crucial for your mental health (Shoubridge et al., 2022).

1236. The bacterium causing Lyme disease, Borrelia burgdorferi, can evade the immune system by changing its surface proteins (Anderson & Brissette, 2021).

1237. Bacteria use a chemical signaling process called quorum sensing to communicate with each other (Waters & Bassler, 2005).

1238. Certain bacteria and fungi are used as biofertilizers in agriculture to enhance plant growth and nutrient uptake (Shahwar et al., 2023). For example, some bacteria fix nitrogen from the atmosphere, and some prevent diseases.

1239. Dodder, a parasitic plant, lacks chlorophyll, roots, and leaves. It extracts nutrients directly from its host plants (Sullivan, 2021b).

1240. In cheesemaking, specific bacteria and molds contribute to the flavor and texture of cheeses during the ripening process (Eberle, 2022).

1241. Plant Parasitic Nematodes are microscopic worms that infect plants and decrease yields (Pulavarty et al., 2021).

1242. Leprosy, caused by the bacteria *Mycobacterium leprae* is one of the oldest recorded diseases in human history (Eichman, 1999). Leprosy symptoms include skin lesions, numbness or loss of sensation in affected areas, muscle weakness, and potential deformities over time

1243. Tapeworm eggs have been discovered in the remains of ancient humans, including mummies (Flammer & Smith, 2020).

1244. Leishmaniasis, affected hundreds of soldiers in the Mediterranean and Middle East, earning it the nickname "Baghdad boil" (Lockwood, 2004).

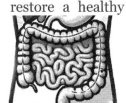

1245. Fecal Microbiota Transplant (FMT), involves transferring fecal matter from a healthy donor to a recipient to restore a healthy balance of gut bacteria (Gupta et al., 2015).

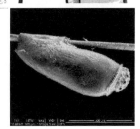

1246. *Ascaris lumbricoides*, or roundworms are responsible for 60,000 deaths annually (Shah & Shahidullah, 2018).

1247. Nits, which are the eggs of head lice, can camouflage themselves to match your hair color (Smith, 2017).

Chapter42: Satisfying Sleep Facts

1248. World Sleep Day is an annual event that is typically observed on the Friday before the Spring Equinox (Pandey, 2023).

1249. The most vivid dreams, including nightmares, occur during REM (Rapid Eye Movement) sleep (Suni & Dimitriu, 2020a).

1250. Sleep talking, or somniloquy is more common in children and tends to decrease with age (Suni & Dimitriu, 2020b).

1251. Those sudden, involuntary muscle contractions that sometimes occur just as you're falling asleep are known as hypnic jerks (Summer, 2021).

1252. While dreaming, the brain actively suppresses certain neurotransmitters, making it challenging to remember dreams (Bahar Gholipour, 2018).

1253. On average, people have four to six dreams every night (Larson, 2020).

1254. The most common position is on the side, followed by back sleeping and stomach sleeping (Singh, 2022).

1255. It's estimated that about 17% of children experience sleepwalking at some point (Arnulf, 2012).

1256. Exploding Head Syndrome is a rare sleep disorder where individuals experience explosions or loud crashes, during the transition from sleep to wakefulness (Nakayama et al., 2021).

1257. Sleep-Related Eating Disorder (SRED) results in people consuming food while asleep, often with no memory of doing so (Cox, 2022).

Chapter 43: Superior Sharks, Whales, Dolphins, and Turtles

1258. Hammerhead sharks have eyes on the sides of their distinctive hammer-shaped heads, giving them a 360-degree view of their surroundings (Yong, 2009b).

1259. Some shark species can reproduce through parthenogenesis, a process where females can produce offspring without mating with a male (Wright, 2021).

1260. Male humpback whales are known for their complex and mysterious songs, which can last up to 20 minutes and be heard for miles (Georgia, 2019).

1261. Some whales, like orcas, engage in spyhopping, where they vertically thrust their heads out of the water to observe their surroundings (A. Wood, 2022).

1262. Some dolphins use sponges to protect their rostrums from sharp shells and rocks while foraging on the ocean floor (Griffiths, 2014).

1263. The Amazon River dolphin, also known as the pink river dolphin, is one of the few dolphin species with a pink coloration (*Amazon river dolphin (Boto) facts*, 2018).

1264. Dolphins give birth tail-first (Littlechild, 2022).

1265. The leatherback sea turtle is the largest turtle species, reaching weights of 2,000 lbs (907 kg) and lengths of 8 ft (2.4 m) (*Seven largest sea turtle species - American Oceans*, 2023).

1266. Hatchling sea turtles use light to navigate from their nest to the ocean. Artificial lights can disorient them, leading them away from the sea (Thums et al., 2016).

1267. A turtle's shell is a fusion of its backbone and ribs. The top part is called the carapace, and the bottom part is the plastron (Kennett, 2020).

1268. A turtle's shell comprises over 50 fused bones (Gilbert, 2008).

1269. The pocket shark, a small deep-sea shark, was only discovered in 2010 in the Gulf of Mexico. It measures just 5.5 in (14 cm) (Johnson, 2019).

1270. A large number of dolphins in captivity are given antidepressants (Farhoud, 2023).

1271. Dolphins and whales can get sunburned (Shapouri, 2012).

1272. Dolphins create and play with underwater bubble rings, a behavior thought to be a form of play or social interaction (Alexander et al., 2021).

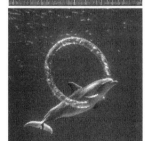

1273.The coloration of a hawksbill sea turtle's shell changes based on water temperature (Jasim, 2023).

1274.Many turtles die from ingesting plastic bags floating in the ocean which they mistake for jellyfish (Newburger, 2020).

1275.The Mata Mata turtle has a flat, camouflaged shell and a long neck resembling fallen leaves, helping it blend seamlessly into its environment (Haines, 2019).

1276.Green sea turtles have symbiotic relationships with fish such as wrasses that feed on organisms that attach themselves to their shells (Steele Miguelez, 2022).

1277.Humpback whales engage in a cooperative feeding technique called "bubble-net" feeding, where they blow a circle of bubbles to trap and concentrate prey (Shaw, 2019).

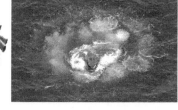

1278.The blue whale's heartbeat can be detected from 2 miles away, and its heart is so massive that a human could theoretically swim through its arteries (Helmenstine, 2023).

1279.Gray whales have a unique dual blowhole arrangement, producing a distinctive heart-shaped blow (Nygreen, 2023).

1280.Sharks cannot produce any sounds and are thought to communicate via body language (Fairing, 2023).

1281.The synchronized hatching of turtle eggs is triggered by environmental factors like temperature ch anges or even the vibrations of nearby hatchlings (Spencer & Janzen, 2011).

1282.Female sea turtles often return to the same beach where they hatched to lay their own eggs, a behavior known as natal homing (Weintraub, 2018).

1283.Similar to tree rings, the growth rings on a turtle's scute (one of the external shell plates) can provide insights into its age and periods of growth (Wilson et al., 2003).

1284.Nurse sharks are nocturnal and gather in groups called "resting aggregations" where they rest on the ocean floor during the day (Allred, 2022).

1285.In 2007, dolphins saved surfer Todd Endris after a shark attack. They surrounded him and kept the shark from hurting him further so he could get back to shore (Celizic, 2007).

1286.In 2020, two kayakers ended up in a humpback whale's mouth! The whale was feeding and engulfed their kayak, dropping them into the water (Selcho, 2022).

1287.Dolphins aren't always nice. There have been reports of dolphins displaying aggressive behavior towards humans or boats (*Are dolphins dangerous? - American Oceans*, 2023).

1288.Some turtles have the ability to breathe out their butts (Baker, 2022a)!

Chapter44: Radical Robots

1289. Unimate, introduced in 1961, is considered the first industrial robot. It was used to transport parts to be welded in a General Motors plant (Norman, n.d.).

1290. The Sojourner rover, part of NASA's Mars Pathfinder mission in 1997, was the first robot to explore the surface of Mars (Howell, 2012).

1291. The da Vinci Surgical System allows surgeons to perform minimally invasive procedures with precision using robotic assistance (Wei & Cerfolio, 2019).

1292. Japan is making progress in developing warehouses fully operated by robots and not humans (Hornyak, 2018).

1293. The world's first ultra-realistic humanoid robot, Ai-Da, can paint just as humans do (Davies, 2022).

1294. The "Meshworm," developed by researchers at MIT, is a soft-bodied robot that moves like an earthworm (Stromberg, 2012b).

1295. MIT's robotic cheetah, a four-legged robot, set a speed record for legged robots by running at 28.3 miles per hour in 2012 (Chu, 2014).

1296. The term "robot" was introduced by Czech writer Karel Čapek in his 1920 play "R.U.R.," which stands for "Rossum's Universal Robots" (Reilly, 2011).

1297. The concept of the "uncanny valley" refers to the discomfort humans feel when robots or animated characters closely resemble but fall just short of appearing completely human (Cherry, 2020).

1298. Joseph F. Engelberger and George C. Devol founded the first robot company in 1956 (Jain, 2019).

Chapter45: Authentic Art and Artist Facts

1299. Leonardo da Vinci, the renowned Renaissance artist, often wrote his notes in reverse to keep them private (Harris, 2023).

1300. The pop art icon Andy Warhol had a collection of wigs that he would wear to create different personas (Newman, 2019). He started his career as a commercial illustrator before transitioning to fine art.

1301. The identity of the street artist Banksy remains a mystery (Duffield, 2023).

1302. In 2018, Banksy's artwork "Girl with a Balloon" was auctioned at Sotheby's. Moments after the winning bid, the artwork began to shred itself through a hidden shredder within the frame (Davidson et al., 2018).

1303. Vincent Van Gogh famously cut off part of his own ear during a mental health crisis in 1888. The severed ear was reportedly given to a woman at a local brothel (Brinkhof, 2023).

1304. Vincent Van Gogh averaged a painting a day and produced nearly 900 works of art over his lifetime (Department of European Paintings, 2019). However, he only sold one painting during his lifetime, "The Red Vineyard."

1305. Pablo Picasso created over 50,000 artworks during his lifetime, including paintings, sculptures, ceramics, and prints.

1306. The surrealist painter Salvador Dalí had an intense fear of grasshoppers (Bai, 2013).

1307. Frida Kahlo wanted to become a doctor but a bus accident left her bedridden with painting as her only escape (Svoboda, 2022).

1308. Pablo Picasso's most expensive painting sold at auction is "Women of Algiers (Version O)," which fetched over $179 million in 2015.

Chapter46: Significant Sport Facts

1309. The largest game of dodgeball involved 6,084 participants and was achieved by the University of California, Irvine in 2012 (Dehaas, 2012).

1310. Extreme ironing competitions involve participants ironing clothes in challenging and extreme locations, such as mountainsides or underwater (Holland, 2020).

1311. In 1976, Janet Guthrie became the first female driver to compete in a NASCAR superspeedway race (Jensen, 2023).

1312. Sumo wrestlers participate in elaborate pre-match rituals, including salt-throwing to purify the ring (Cloutman, 2019).

1313. Synchronized swimming was originally called "water ballet" and made its Olympic debut in 1984 (Penzel, 2012).

1314. American sprinter Jim Hines became the first man to run the 100 meters in under 10 seconds during the 1968 Summer Olympics (Andres, 2023).

1315. The highest marathon on Earth is the Tenzing-Hillary Everest Marathon. It starts at the Everest Base Camp at an altitude of 17,600 ft (5,364 m) and finishes at Namche ft/3,440 m) (Bywater, 2023).

1316. Kathrine Switzer became the first woman to officially run the Boston Marathon in 1967 (Kotecha, 2021).

1317. Shohei Ohtani signed a Major League Baseball contract with the Los Angeles Dodgers for $700 million, making it the largest contract signed to date (Wells, 2023).

1318. The first official basketball game was played on December 21, 1891, at the International YMCA Training School in Springfield, Massachusetts (McCuaig, 2023).

1319. Soviet gymnast Larisa Latynina holds the record for the most Olympic medals won by a female, with 18 medals between 1956 and 1964 (Dunlap, 2021).

1320. The first marathon was run in 1896 and the winner, Spiridon Louis from Greece, drank alcohol to get him through the race (Blakemore, 2023).

1321. The World Golf Hall of Fame includes a category for caddies, recognizing their significant contributions to the sport (Wulf, 2013).

1322. Quidditch, the fictional sport from the Harry Potter series, has been adapted into a real sport played on broomsticks (Ali, 2021).

1323. The record for the most Olympic appearances is held by Canadian equestrian Ian Millar, who competed in ten Olympic Games from 1972 to 2012 (Nair, 2021).

1324. The longest tennis match in history took place at Wimbledon in 2010. John Isner and Nicolas Mahut played for 11 hours and 5 minutes over 3 days.

1325. The World Ice Golf Championship has taken place annually since 1999 in Uummannaq, Greenland (Kelly, 2014).

1326. Rugby supposedly originated in 1823 when William Webb Ellis picked up the ball during a soccer game and ran with it (Aylwin, 2019). 1327. Aaron Yoder set the world record for the fastest mile run backward, completing it in 5 minutes and 54.25 seconds in 2015 (Dupere, 2020).

1328. Underwater hockey, also known as Octopush, is a sport played at the bottom of a swimming pool (Neilson, 2023).

1329. Oscar Swahn, a Swedish shooter, holds the record as the oldest Olympic medalist at the age of 72 (Belam, 2021).

1330. Tyrone "Muggsy" Bogues, standing at 5 ft 3 in (160 cm), is the shortest player in NBA history (Ash, 2023).

1331. Basketball legend Michael Jordan briefly retired from the NBA in 1993 to pursue a baseball career (Piccotti, 2021). He scored 88 hits and 3 homeruns.

1332. Blind soccer, also known as five-a-side football, is played by visually impaired athletes who wear blindfolds. The ball contains bells to help players locate it (Ronald, 2022).

1333. Table tennis played a role in diplomatic relations between the United States and China during the early 1970s, leading to improved relations in what became known as "Ping Pong Diplomacy" (Andrewsb, 2018).

1334. Cy Young pitched the first perfect game in baseball history in 1904 (Brew, 2023). A perfect game in baseball is when a pitcher faces and retires all 27 batters without allowing any to reach base.

1335. The 1968 Winter Olympics was the first time an Olympic mascot was used. It was a little man on skis called Shuss.

1336. Chess-boxing combines chess and boxing to form its own sport. Participants alternate between rounds of chess and boxing until a checkmate or knockout occurs (Dunlap, 2022).

1337. Toe wrestling is a sport where two participants compete to pin each other's foot down while sitting face to face (Kim, 2023).

1338. Yukigassen is a competitive snowball fight sport that originated in Japan. Two teams of seven work to dodge snowballs and capture the other team's flag (Asghar, 2021).

1339. Serena Williams has 23 Grand Slam singles titles, the most by any player in the Open Era (Fleming, 2022).

Chapter47: Completely Crazy Beliefs From The Past

1340.Left-handed people were thought to be associated with the devil (Rothman, 2015).

1341.Alchemists sought the Philosopher's Stone, an object believed to turn metals into gold. It was never found, but the search gave rise to modern chemistry and metallurgy (Pruitt, 2018). 1342.In the 18th century, people believed that rubbing onions and honey on their heads would help cure male baldness (Homan, 2019).

1343.The ancient Greeks believed health was influenced by balancing the four humors in the body: blood, phlegm, black bile, and yellow bile (Prabhu, 2022).

1344.Various cultures believed in the existence of a Fountain of Youth that could reverse the aging process (Drye, 2017).

1345.In the past, people believed that a full moon could induce madness or lunacy, a belief reflected in the term "lunatic" (Stanborough, 2020).

1346.In medieval Europe, people believed in changelings—supernatural beings swapped for human babies by fairies (Gray, 2020). 1347.Despite overwhelming evidence to the contrary, some individuals still believe in a flat Earth (Furze, 2019).

1348.Ancient Egyptians believed the sun was a solar deity riding a chariot across the sky during the day and sailing through the underworld at night (Haikal, 2019).

1349.Seeking guidance from oracles, such as the Oracle of Delphi in ancient Greece, was a common practice for decision-making (Hayward, 2020).

1350.Claims of individuals time traveling from the future occasionally surface, with some even sharing supposed evidence or predictions (Eddy, 2018).

1351.In the 1960s, the existence of polywater—a purported new form of water with abnormal properties—was suggested but later debunked (Stromberg, 2013). It claimed to have boiling point of 150℃, when normal water has 100℃. 1352.In the 19th century, chewing gum was believed to alleviate a variety of health issues (Sands, 2023).

1353.Superstition held that the hand of a criminal who had been hanged had healing properties (Davies & Matteoni, 2015).

1354.Thomas Edison attempted to create a device to communicate with the dead, known as the "spirit phone" (Zarrelli, 2016).

1355.It was believed that dead bodies must be carried out of the house feet first to prevent them from looking back at their homes and the people in them (Rodgers, 2016).

1356. Monarchs were believed to have the power to heal scrofula (a form of tuberculosis) by touching the afflicted (Turrell, 1999).

1357. A belief that is still held today is that there must be ravens in the Tower of London otherwise Britain will fall (Nelson, 2023). This belief is so ingrained that special measures are taken by the country to make sure ravens are in the Tower, such as their wings being clipped so they can't fly away.

1358. Ancient Egyptians believed that certain animals, like cats, were incarnations of the Gods which is why they were treated with such respect (Andrews, 2018a).

1359. In 16th and 17th century England, it was believed that placing a dead cat within the walls of your home would ward off evil (Willis, 2022).

1360. Mental illness was often misunderstood, and exorcisms were sometimes performed to expel supposed demons (Trethowan, 1976).

1361. In medieval times, people thought that elves were to blame for hiccups (Tung, 2015).

1362. Ancient Romans believed that breaking a mirror would bring seven years of bad luck because mirrors were thought to hold a piece of the soul.

1363. There was once a Whale Hotel in Australia that facilitated people lying in the carcasses of dead whales to treat their arthritis.

1364. In the Victorian era, people would cover the mirrors in a house where someone died. They did not want their spirit to get stuck in them (Rodgers, 2016).

1365. People believed that the appearance of plants indicated their medicinal uses. For example, a heart-shaped leaf would be used for heart ailments (Simon, 2014a).

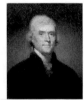

1366. In France, it was considered bad luck to place bread upside down on the table, as it was associated with death.

1367. The Curse of the Ninth is a superstition that composers who wrote a ninth symphony would die, popularized after Beethoven's death (Waters, 2018).

1368. Thomas Jefferson, the 3rd president of the United States, believed that meat should be eaten as a condiment for vegetables (Mendelsohn, 2012).

1369. Napoleon Bonaparte was reportedly afraid of cats and believed that his fate was tied to encountering them (Harvey, 2015).

1370. In Hungary and other countries, sitting at the corner of a table means you won't get married for seven years.

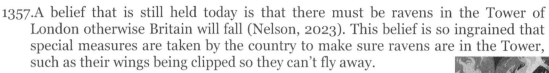
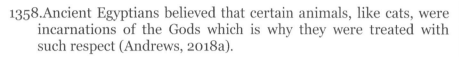
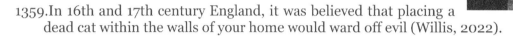
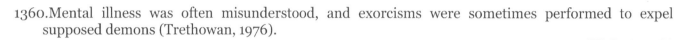
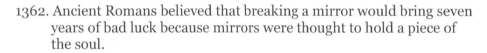
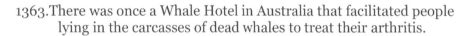
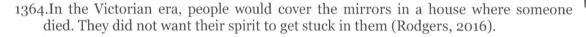
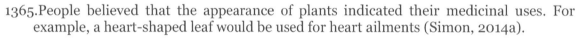

Chapter48: Hearty Holidays and Celebrations

1371. On the last Monday of January, enthusiasts celebrate the joy of popping bubble wrap (Parsons, 2023).

1372. National Nothing Day is celebrated on January 16th. This day encourages people to do absolutely nothing and embrace the art of relaxation (Handler, 2019).

1373. On the first Saturday of April, cities worldwide host massive pillow fights in public spaces (Glanfield, 2014).

1374. December 8th is Pretend to be a Time Traveler Day. Participants act as if they are time travelers visiting from the past or future (Gigoux, 2007).

1375. In Lopburi, Thailand, monkeys are treated to a lavish buffet of fruits and treats during the Monkey Buffet Festival (Kamolvattanavith, 2022). 1376. La Tomatina in Buñol, Spain, is a festival where participants engage in a massive tomato fight. It is estimated that hundreds of tons of tomatoes are consumed during the festival.

1377. Celebrated on December 5th, St. Nicholas Day is when children place shoes by the fireplace to get filled with treats or small gifts (Rodriguez, 2022).

1378. On November 5th, Brits commemorate the foiled Gunpowder Plot by burning effigies of Guy Fawkes on bonfires and enjoying fireworks (Street, 2023).

1379. Día de los Santos Inocentes in Spain is similar to April Fools' Day. This holiday on December 28th involves playing pranks and jokes (Oppliger, 2023).

1380. The International Balloon Fiesta in Albuquerque, New Mexico, is the largest hot air balloon festival in the world, attracting around 500 of colorful balloons and thousands of spectators each year.

Chapter49: Gloriously Green Facts

1381. In 2022, 12% of the world's power was generated from solar and wind (Meredith, 2023).

1382. China is the leading global producer of solar panels, generating about 80% of the world's total production (Hawkins, 2023).

1383. The cost of solar panels has dropped by over 89% in the last decade.

1384. Recycling a ton of paper can save approximately 17 trees and 7,000 gallons of water (West, 2020). That's roughly what 14,000 people drink each year on average.

1385. The world generated approximately 59.4 million metric tons of electronic waste in 2022 (Tiseo, 2023).

1386. It is estimated that by 2050, there will be more plastic in the oceans than fish by weight (Wearden, 2018).

1387. A leaky faucet dripping once per second can waste more than 3,000 gallons of water annually (*Fix a leak week*, 2017). That's roughly what 6,000 people drink each year on average.

1388. The ozone layer is recovering at a rate of about 1–3% per decade since 2000 (Harvey, 2018). The gas of fluorinated compounds, for example used in refrigerators, were destroying the ozone layer, and people were concerned about harmful UV light that could come from the ozone hall. But thanks to the effort of restricting their use, the layer is recovering.

1389. Sustainable tourism focuses on minimizing the environmental impact of travel while supporting local economies and cultures (Boado, 2020). The impact include air pollution, water consumption, waste generation, etc.

1390. The power potential from the world's oceans is estimated to be around 20,000–80,000 terawatt-hours per year which is 100–400% of current world demands (Cho, 2017).

Chapter50: Incredibly Impressive Occupations

1391.In medieval England, a town crier was a person who made public announcements in the streets before newspapers were widespread (Castelow, 2017).

1392.Rat catchers in the early 18th century were hired to catch and control rat populations in urban areas (Goddard, 2012).

1393.An Ice Cutter was responsible for cutting and harvesting ice from frozen lakes for refrigeration before modern refrigerators in the 19th century (Singh, 2023).

1394.In ancient Greece, there was a trumpet player who would be hired to play at sacrifices (Tarantino, 2023).

1395.During the Civil War, a Powder Monkey was the name given to little boys who helped with loading and handling gunpowder on naval ships (Baer & De Luce, 2019).

1396.In the 18th and 19th centuries, Leech Collectors gathered leeches for medical use (Baer & De Luce, 2019).

1397.In medieval times, the person who was hired to flush out game during a hunt was called a Battuere (Killgrove, 2018).

1398.Candle Clock Makers had to craft candles in 10th century England that burned at specific rates to measure time (Rogers, 2011).

1399.A Pure Finder in the Victorian era had to collect dog poop to be used by tanners (Deron, 2015).

1400.A Knacker is someone who collects and renders animal carcasses. The occupation is still valid today (Bathurst, 2021). Knackers play a crucial role in animal carcass disposal, preventing disease spread and recycling waste into useful products, supporting environmental health.

1401.Petticoat Inspectors enforced laws regulating the length of women's skirts in the early 20th century (Pliley, 2013).

1402.People would hire mourners in Ancient Egypt and it is an occupation still available today (Dicken, 2021)!

1403.A Link Boy would guide people through the dark streets with a torch in the 17th century (Hamey, 2013).

1404.Funeral mutes in the Victorian era had to stand vigil at the entrance of the house of the deceased and lead the funeral procession (Tiller, 2016).

1405. The ancient Romans had urine collectors who gathered and sold urine for various purposes, including textile production and tanning (Mohi Kumar, 2013).

1406. A Phrenologist in the 19th century studied the bumps on people's heads to determine their personalities (Baer & De Luce, 2019).

1407. Lice picking is a legitimate and lucrative occupation (O'Brien, 2016). There are some information claiming around over $90,000 a year, although it should largely depend on the conditions.

1408. Hackers were what woodcutters were called before they were replaced by machines (Ladd, 2017).

1409. Lungs were employed in alchemist shops in the 16th and 17th centuries to keep the fires burning (Ladd, 2017).

1410. In ancient Greece, Bematists used to measure the distance between places using their steps (Scott, 2023).

1411. It was the job of herb strewers to throw fragrant herbs in rooms in houses and castles to mask strong odors early in the 16th century (Sheridan, 2022).

1412. Nomenclators in Ancient Rome had to remember people's names so that they could whisper them to their bosses (Meddings, 2017).

1413. A person called an Inspector of Nuisance was employed to sniff out bad smells in public otherwise deemed nuisances in the mid-19th century (Samson, 2020)

1414. Dog whippers would prevent dogs from interrupting church services.

1415. Professional Snugglers or Cuddlers can be hired nowadays for cuddles.

1416. An Ocularist designs and fits custom-made prosthetic eyes (Khandekar et al., 2020).

1417. You can now hire a professional Mermaid/Merman for events and parties.

1418. Crime Scene Cleaners clean and sanitize crime scenes after investigations (Layton, 2023).

1419. A Lego Master Builder is someone who constructs large-scale sculptures and displays using Lego bricks (Hinds, 2020).

1420. The person who creates sound effects for movies and TV shows is called a Foley Artist (Ulea & Van Rouveroy, 2023).

1421. A Futurist or Futurologist is someone who predicts and analyzes future trends and developments in various fields (Parsons, n.d.).

Chapter51: Super Spies and Espionage

1422. The United Kingdom has domestic and foreign intelligence agencies known as MI5 and MI6, respectively (Deedes, 2004).

1423. Kim Philby was a high-ranking MI6 officer and a Soviet double agent part of the Cambridge Spy Ring (Leake, 2022). He was betraying secrets to the KGB while working for MI6.

1424. The Cuban Five were Cuban intelligence officers arrested in the U.S. for spying on anti-Castro groups (Prieto, 2020).

1425. The Enigma Machine was a typewriter-like machine used by the Germans during WWII. Allied codebreakers, including Alan Turing, cracked their codes (Markuson, 2021).

1426. The Insectothopter is a CIA-developed miniature drone resembling a dragonfly, intended for surveillance (Morton, 2015).

1427. Soviet spy Rudolf Abel used a hollowed-out nickel to exchange microfilm in the U.S. (Federal Bureau of Investigation, n.d.).

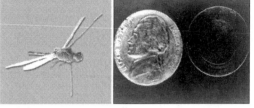

1428. Microdots are tiny photographs or documents reduced to the size of a dot and hidden on objects or within other documents, used by allies and Germans during WWII. The image is an envelope with microdots sent by German spies in Mexico to Lisbon, intercepted by Allies. You can see the whole documents by using magnifiers.

1429. The infiltration of the FBI by Soviet spies damaged U.S. intelligence for years (Cohen & McLaughlin, 2018).

1430 Cameras disguised as everyday objects, such as pens, buttons, or eyeglasses for covert photography are used by CIA. 1431.Soviet spy Richard Miller was the first FBI agent to be arrested for espionage in 1985 (Mirzai, 2023b).

1432. Eddie Chapman (Agent Zigzag) was a British double agent during WWII, he worked for both the Germans and British intelligence (Kross, 2020).

1433. During WWII, number stations were used to broadcast sequences of numbers which were actually instructions to agents and soldiers (Fox, 2010).

1434. Alger Hiss, a U.S. State Department official, was accused of being a Soviet spy, in the 1940s but was only convicted in the 1950s after he denied being a spy (Hadley, 2020).

1435. The Battle of Jutland in WWI was sparked by British naval intelligence's interception of German naval codes which detailed luring the British fleet (Osborne, 2014).

1436. The Zimmermann Telegram, intercepted by British intelligence in WWI, was a proposal to Mexico to form an alliance with Germany to attack the U.S. (Andrews, 2018c).

1437. The Stasi (Ministry for State Security) was East Germany's secret police. They kept information on individuals from the public and used it to control what they said or did (Amnesty International, 2015). It maintained one of the most extensive spy networks in history, with over 91,000 full-time employees and informants.

1438. Dubbed the "Granny Spy," Melita Norwood spied for the Soviets in the UK for over 40 years (Hastings, 2008).

1439. The Eiffel Tower's wireless telegraph transmitter was used to jam German communications during the 1914 Battle of Marnes (Specktor, 2018).

1440. The U.S. Navy trained dolphins and sea lions to protect naval officers against threats in the water and locate objects (Fuentes, 2022).

1441. The CIA was inspired by James Bond writer and former spy, Ian Fleming in the creation of some spy gadgets (Ellyatt, 2013).

1442. A pigeon named Cher Ami saved the lives of nearly 200 soldiers surrounded by enemies during WWI by delivering a request for support (Bieniek, 2017). Although being shot on the way, she kept flying to the headquarter 25 miles (40km) away and delivered the message.

1443. There is a beluga whale named Hvaldamir who is thought to be a Russian spy. He has been spotted in Norway and Sweden (Treisman, 2023).

1444. Moe Berg was a Major League Baseball player who served as a spy during WWII, providing intelligence on German scientific developments (Clary, 2023).

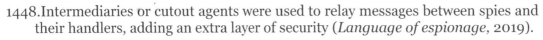

1445. Operation Cornflakes saw Allied forces drop fake German mail to demoralize German troops during WWII (Barrett, 2020).

1446. French intelligence agents sank the Greenpeace ship in New Zealand in 1985 to prevent protests against French nuclear tests (Willsher, 2015). 1447. Dead drops are secret locations used to exchange information or materials between spies without direct contact. Dead drop spikes are covert devices used to hide messages or items in public places. They consist of hollow tubes buried in the ground, accessible only to individuals who know their location.

1448. Intermediaries or cutout agents were used to relay messages between spies and their handlers, adding an extra layer of security (*Language of espionage*, 2019).

1449. The U.S. banned postal chess during WWII because it feared it was being used to send encoded messages to its enemies (Oberhaus, 2017). Postal chess is a chess game played by sending moves through mail, allowing players to compete over long distances.

1450. In the French Revolutionary War, spies used balloons with observation platforms for aerial reconnaissance (Himmelman, 2023).

1451. A cipher disk is a cryptographic device used to encode and decode secret messages, developed in 1470 in Italy. To use a cipher disk, first, determine a key letter or symbol alignment for encoding and decoding messages. Then, rotate the outer and inner disks so that the chosen letters or symbols correspond on both. Write your message using these matched pairs. To decode, align the disks to reveal the original message.

Chapter52: Astonishing Accidents, Crimes, and Scams

1452. Charles Ponzi's investment fraud scheme in 1922 gave rise to the term "Ponzi scheme" (Probasco, 2022). It is a fraudulent investment scam that promises high returns to investors, paying earlier investors with funds from new investors rather than generating legitimate profits. Eventually, the scheme collapses when new investments dry up, leaving many investors with significant losses.

1453. Financier Bernie Madoff orchestrated the largest Ponzi scheme in history, defrauding investors of billions of dollars (Hayes, 2020a). Some estimates the loss to investors can be as much as $18 billion.

1454. Two Boeing 747s collided on the runway at Tenerife Airport in 1977 causing the deadliest aviation accident in history (Hayward & Karuwa, 2021).

1455. In 1971, a man hijacked a plane, received a ransom, and then parachuted away. The man gave the name D.B. Cooper when he boarded but neither he nor money was ever found (Zurowski, 2023).

1456. In 2015, a group of elderly thieves, aged between 58 and 70 years old, broke into a safe deposit box facility in London, stealing millions of dollars in valuables (Seal, 2016).

1457. The son of aviator Charles Lindbergh was kidnapped in 1932, leading to a high-profile investigation (Braden, 2022).

1458. The Pink Panthers are a network of jewel thieves responsible for high-profile heists around the world (Varady, 2023). One of the most famous heists by the group is the heist of the jewelry store Harry Winston in Paris on 2008, stealing over $100 million worth of jewelries.

1459. The Great Smog of London in 1952 resulted in thousands of deaths, and some argue that industrial pollution combined with weather patterns contributed to the disaster (Blakemore, 2022).

1460. In 2003, thieves stole over $100 million worth of diamonds from a safe deposit box in Antwerp, making it the largest diamond heist in history (Davis, 2009).

1461. During the late 1960s and early 1970s, the Zodiac Killer operated in northern California. The killer taunted law enforcement and the media with cryptic letters and ciphers but was never found (Kaufman, 2023).

Chapter53: Spooky Snake and Vulture Facts

Snakes

1462. Snake venom varies greatly, and some species have venom that can contain hundreds of bioactive compounds (Oliveira et al., 2022).

1463. Snakes have flexible jaws, allowing them to eat prey larger than their head by dislocating their jaws (MacDonald, 2019).

1464. The anaconda is the heaviest snake in the world, capable of weighing over 500 pounds (227 kg).

1465. Some snakes have tiny, non-functional limbs, remnants of their evolutionary past. These are called vestigial limbs (Kennedy, 2020).

1466. Snake eggs are permeable, allowing for gas exchange through the shell. Some species even "breathe" through their eggs (Legendre et al., 2022). 1467. Some snakes can change color, like the chameleon snake, adapting to their surroundings for camouflage (Holder, 2022).

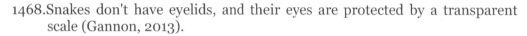

1468. Snakes don't have eyelids, and their eyes are protected by a transparent scale (Gannon, 2013).

1469. Some snakes have keel scales, which provide traction and aid in movement (Ward, 2022a).

1470. Snakes have specialized teeth called egg teeth to help them slit open the egg during hatching (Hermyt et al., 2017).

1471. Occasionally, snakes are born with two heads, a condition known as bicephaly. These two heads may not always cooperate, leading to challenges in hunting and coordination (Salleh, 2018).

1472. St. Patrick is celebrated for chasing all the snakes out of Ireland, but it is just one island out of many that did not have any snakes (Pruitt, 2020).

1473. The ouroboros, a snake eating its own tail, is an ancient symbol representing cyclicality, eternity, and the cycle of life, death, and rebirth (Othman, 2023).

1474. It is possible for snakes to strike you underwater (Purser, 2011). Also, sea snakes can swim at around 10-15 mph (16-24 kph), which is faster than the human's world record for swimming.

1475. Snakes can regurgitate their food if they feel threatened or stressed, conserving energy for escape (Banu, 2023).

Vultures

1476. Vultures are among the highest-flying birds, with some species, like the Rüppell's griffon vulture, recorded at altitudes of over 37,000 feet (11,278 meters) (Weisberger, 2016).

1477. Vultures are often seen in groups, called a wake, committee, or kettle, depending on what they're doing (Hall, 2023).

1478. The population of African vultures has decreased by 97% in the last 50 years (Chebet, 2023).

1479. The white-backed vulture is facing a significant decline in numbers, primarily due to poisoning from the veterinary drug diclofenac (Oaks et al., 2004).

1480. Egyptian vultures have been observed using tools, such as rocks, to crack open ostrich eggs (Yong, 2011).

1481. Old World vultures primarily find carrion by sight, whereas New World vultures often rely on their sense of smell (Felmore, 2019).

1482. In 2021, a Griffin Vulture flew into an electricity pylon in Alberquerque, Spain, got electrocuted, and started a wildfire (Vulture Conservation Foundation, 2021).

1483. Vultures excrete a strong, corrosive uric acid that helps sanitize their legs and feet after walking through carrion (Menser, 2017).

1484. Vultures engage in sunbathing to kill bacteria on their plumage and to regulate their body temperature (Ellis, 2019).

1485. Vultures have a large crop, allowing them to consume and store a significant amount of food to regurgitate later for their young (Felmore, 2019).

1486. New world vultures do not have a vocal organ like other birds. They can only make limited sounds (Ward, 2022b).

1487. White storks and vultures sometimes form mixed-species foraging groups, taking advantage of each other's abilities to locate food (Wong, 2011).

1488. Bearded vultures are known for their unique feeding behavior, which involves dropping bones from a height to access the marrow (Hellickson, n.d.).

1489. You might think that vultures are bland, but the king vulture, found in Central and South America, has strikingly vibrant skin with colors like orange, red, and purple on its head and neck (B. Haines, 2019).

1490. Vultures have specialized blood vessels in their heads that help regulate body temperature (Ward et al., 2008).

1491. Vultures aren't as gross as you would imagine. They will take a bath after a meal if there is water available (Hay, 2013).

Chapter54: Running, Swimming, Flying, Climbing

1492. Sloths can swim! Actually they can swim well that there was a case where sloth was observed swimming in the sea to reach for a mangrove forest.

1493. Wild boars can swim too! Wild boars were found swimming from the mainland to the islands in Japan. At that time, local farmers of the islands were wondering who were eating their crops such as oranges, and later the coast guard ships found them swimming in the sea for roughly 30 km! They were coming to eat their crops.

1494. So can kangaroos! There were cases where kangaroos were swimming the coast of Australia.

1495. Elephants can swim too! While Asian elephants weigh around 2,000 to 5,500 kg (4,400 to can float in the water, use their trunks as snorkels, and crawl their legs and swim!

1496. Ibexes, a type of mountain goat, can climb near-vertical cliffs and can even take rest there. They are found climbing and sitting on the dam wall in Italy to lick the secreting salt.

1497. Bears can climb too! In fact there are many cases where bears were climbing near-vertical mountain cliffs.

1498. Flying fish can jump out of the sea and glide for considerable distances, sometimes reaching heights of several meters and covering distances of over 200 m using their fins.

1499. Flying squids can also "fly" for several meters by squirting water, using the same principle as jet propulsion.

Chapter55: Lightning Speed Facts

1500.The fastest bicycle speed ever recorded was achieved by Denise Mueller-Korenek in 2018, hitting 294kph (184mph) (as of 2023). She was able to achieve this by riding her bicycle closely behind a leading car that not only towed her till the top speed but also worked as a windshield to reduce the drag.

1501.The fastest soccer shot ever recorded was achieved by Francisco Javier Galán Marín, a Spanish footballer in 2019, kicked the ball at a speed of 129 km/h (80.1 mph) (fastest as of 2023).

1502.The fastest punch by humans ever recorded was achieved by Keith Liddell. His punch recorded 45 mph(72kph). He was not only a qualified boxer for the summer Olympics in London 2012, but also a mathematician and author.

1503.The fastest golf shot ever recorded was achieved by Ryan Winther of the United States in 2017. Winther's shot was recorded at a speed of 220 mph (354 kph) (fastest as of 2023).

1504.The fastest skateboard speed(downhill) was achieved by Peter Connolly from UK in 2017, reaching 146.73 km/h (91.17 mph) (fastest as of 2023).

1505.The fastest recorded speed for a ping pong (table tennis) ball was achieved by Alexander Karakasevic of Serbia in 2015. His shot recorded at 138 kph (85.7 mph) (fastest as

1506.The fastest swim by humans was achieved by César Cielo, a Brazilian Olympic swimmer. He swam the 50-meter freestyle with a time of 20.91 seconds in 2009(8.6kph/5.3mph) (fastest as of 2023).

1507.The sailfish is the fastest fish in the ocean that are capable of swimming at speeds of up to 68 mph (110 kph) in short bursts. That is roughly 12 times faster than César Cielo, the fastest human swimmer.

1508.Usain Bolt of Jamaica holds the title of the fastest human sprinter ever recorded. Bolt set the world records for both the men's 100 meters and 200 meters sprint events. He achieved his world record time of 9.58 seconds in the 100 meters in 2009 (37.5kph/23.4mph).

1509.Sloths run(crawl) the ground at around 0.15-0.3mph (0.24-0.48kph) on average. In a theoretical world where both can keep running at their top speeds, Usain will finish 78-157 times of 100m runs before a sloth finishes one.

1510.On the other hand, capybaras are the largest rodents in the world, native to South America. Despite their hefty size, they can run surprisingly quickly, reaching speeds of up to 22mph (35 kph), which is comparable to Usain Bolt's world record.

1511. Nerve conduction speeds can vary but some nerve's signal can reach m/s(432kph or 275 mph).

1512 Tiger beetle is one of the fastest insect on land. It can run at around 5.6 mph (9 kph) in short bursts, which is comparable to an average man's walking speed(around 5.6 mph or 9kph).

1513. Woodpeckers can peck woods at around 20 times per second!

1514. F1 cars can accelerate from 0 to 60 mph (97 kph) in around 2 seconds, making them incredibly quick off the line.

1515. The fastest flying insect is considered to be dragonflies, capable of reaching up to 30 - 60 kph (19 - 37 mph).

1516. The fastest recorded heartbeat in a mammal belongs to the Etruscan shrew, with a heart rate of over 1,500 beats per minute.

Chapter55: Paranormal

1517. While some crop circles are hoaxes, others remain unexplained, leading to theories about extraterrestrial or paranormal origins (Radford, 2017).

1518. Electronic Voice Phenomena (EVP) involves capturing unexplained voices on audio recordings, often during paranormal investigations (Rojas, 2011).

1519. The Mothman, a creature reportedly seen in Point Pleasant, West Virginia, is associated with a series of tragic events in the 1960s (Vickery, 2021).

1520. Spontaneous human combustion is a rare phenomenon where a person allegedly catches fire without an external heat source (Watson & Mancini, 2005).

1521. Charles Hickson and Calvin Parker claimed they were abducted by aliens in 1973 while fishing near Pascagoula, Mississippi (Brockell, 2019).

1522. Skinwalker Ranch in Utah gained notoriety for numerous reported paranormal events, including UFO sightings, strange creatures, and unexplained lights.

1523. Sightings of a creature resembling a werewolf have been reported in Michigan, particularly in the 20th century, giving rise to the myth of the Michigan Dogman (Fox, 2021).

1524. Many people who claim to have been abducted by aliens suffer trauma from their experiences. Their accounts were obtained through hypnotic regression to prove their validity (Cromie, 2003).

1525. Ed and Lorraine Warren, paranormal investigators, claimed to have encountered a haunted doll named Annabelle, inspiring the "Annabelle" film series (DaRosa, 2021).

1526. Sarah Winchester, widow of the inventor of the Winchester rifle, built a sprawling, maze-like mansion with staircases leading to nowhere to confuse ghosts she believed were haunting her (Edmonds, 2008).

Chapter56: Probability and Luck

1527. The infinite monkey theorem suggests that given infinite time, a monkey randomly pressing keys on a typewriter would eventually produce the complete works of Shakespeare (Bellos, 2023).

1528. The odds of dying in a car crash are higher than many people perceive, with approximately a 101:1 chance over a lifetime (Lu, 2023).

1529. Despite the extremely low odds of winning, lottery ticket sales often increase during times of economic hardship (Blalock et al., 2007).

1530. In a group of just 57 people, there's a 99% chance that two people share the same birthday (Choi, 2022a).

1531. Scoring a hole-in-one in golf is a rare feat, with odds estimated to be around 1 in 12,000 for amateur golfers (Auclair, 2018).

1532. Contrary to the saying, lightning can strike the same place more than once. In fact, it often does due to geographic and meteorological factors (*Lightning facts and information*, 2009).

1533. Joan Ginther won multi-million-dollar jackpots in the Texas Lottery four times (Weber, 2010).

1534. In a standard deck of 52 cards, the probability of being dealt a royal flush in poker is 1 in 649,740 (Taylor, 2012). Royal flush is the highest-ranking poker hand, consisting of a ten, jack, queen, king, and ace of the same suit.

1535. Job interviews involve an element of luck, as the success of the interview can depend on factors beyond one's control, such as the interviewer's mood or the competition (Mandel, 2019).

1536. In some cases, athletes born in the earlier months of the year have statistically higher chances of excelling in sports (Wigmore, 2021).

Conclusion

"Education is the kindling of a flame, not the filling of a vessel." –Socrates

Just as Socrates said above, I hope that this book has ignited a flame that encourages you to continue learning facts about the world. There will never come a point where you will know them all, which means there is always something new to discover!

In this book, we have covered a variety of different topics but it is just the tip of the iceberg. Be sure to check out the other books in the series if you want to learn even more because this book may have come to an end, but I am sure that this is just the start of your journey! Keep reading, stay curious, and keep learning!

References

For the sources of each fact and images cite, please read the QR code below and download the pdf.

Made in the USA
Coppell, TX
09 July 2024

34456097R00061